CREDIT SECRETS

3 in 1

Boost Your FICO Score By 200 Points in Less Than 30 Days, Without Hiring Credit Repair Agencies. 609 Letter Templates Included + Bonus: 10 Secrets The Experts Don't Share

NEIL HACK

© **Copyright 2021 by Neil Hack - All rights reserved.**

This document is geared towards providing exact and reliable information in regard to the topic and issue covered.

From a Declaration of Principles which was accepted and approved equally by a Committee of the American Bar Association and a Committee of Publishers and Associations.

In no way is it legal to reproduce, duplicate, or transmit any part of this document in either electronic means or in printed format. All rights reserved.

The information provided herein is stated to be truthful and consistent, in that any liability, in terms of inattention or otherwise, by any usage or abuse of any policies, processes, or directions contained within is the solitary and utter responsibility of the recipient reader. Under no circumstances will any legal responsibility or blame be held against the publisher for any reparation, damages, or monetary loss due to the information herein, either directly or indirectly.

Respective authors own all copyrights not held by the publisher.

The information herein is offered for informational purposes solely and is universal as so. The presentation of the information is without contract or any type of guarantee assurance.

The trademarks that are used are without any consent, and the publication of the trademark is without permission or backing by the trademark owner. All trademarks and brands within this book are for clarifying purposes only and are owned by the owners themselves, not affiliated with this document.

Table of Contents

BOOK 1 CREDIT SCORE HACKS *15*

Introduction *16*

Chapter 1:   The FICO Score *24*

    What is a FICO Score? 24

    How Do You Check Your Credit Score? 25

    What is a Good Credit Score? 26

    Increasing Your Fico Credit Score 27

    Access to Best Credit Cards 28

    Easy Access to Loan 29

    Lower Interest Rates on Loans 29

    Easy Approval for Rental of Houses and Apartment 29

    Better Job Applications 30

    Negotiating Power 30

Chapter 2:   10 Credit Repair Myths *31*

    Myth 1: Closing Credit Accounts Will Help Your Score 31

    Myth 2: You Can Increase Your Score by Asking Your Credit Card Company to Lower Your Limits 32

    Myth 3: You Need to Pay Interest to Obtain a Good Credit Score 33

    Myth 4: Your Closed Accounts Should Indicate "Closed by Consumer," Or They Will Hurt Your Score 34

    Myth 5: Credit Counselling Is Way Worse Than Bankruptcy 34

    Myth 6: Pre-Employment Screens Use Credit Scores 35

Myth 7: The Worth of Your Account Age Will Be Lost When a Card Is Closed 36

Myth 8: Once You Ruin Your Credit, You'll Never Rebuild It 36

Myth 9: Checking Your Report Will Harm Your Score 37

Myth 10: Bankruptcy Protection Will Be Excellent for Those Who Have Large Amounts of Debt 37

Chapter 3: *What is Bad for My Credit Score* *39*

Multiple Inquiries 39

Being Over-Extended 40

Too Many Cards Applications 40

Cancelling Cards 41

Late Payment Loans 41

Non-Paying Bill/Mortgage Payment Loans 41

Chapter 4: *6 Steps to Repair Bad Credit Score* *42*

Step 1: Review Your Credit Score Regularly 42

Step 2: Pay All Your Bills on Time 42

Step 3: Do Not Apply for a Loan Ever Again! 44

Step 4: Get Loans from Banks, Not Credit Unions 45

Step 5: Use Your Credit Cards Wisely 46

Step 6: If You Can't Pay Off Your Debt, Pay It Off! 47

Chapter 5: *The 10 Secrets the Experts Don't Share* *49*

1. Pay Bills on Time 49
2. Challenge Late Fees 50
3. Set Up Payment Alerts 50
4. Keep Your Older Accounts Open 51

5. Forget About Older Derogatory Accounts 51
   6. Stop Buying Things on Credit 52
   7. Mind Your Balances 52
   8. Pay Down Your Debt at Lower Costs 53
   9. Mix Up Your Credit 54
   10. Limit New Credit Applications 54
   Note: Do Not Forget to Monitor Credit Activity 55

Chapter 6: Mistakes You Should Avoid When Dealing with Your Credit Score 57

   Paying Just the Minimum 57
   Ignoring Your Billing Statement 57
   Canceling Your Credit Card 58
   Paying Late 58
   Loaning Your Credit Card 59
   Not Knowing Your Credit Card Terms 59
   Letting Your Card Get Charged-Off 60
   Applying for Too Much Credit 60
   Maxing Your Card Out 60
   Getting Pressured into Accepting New Cards 61
   Sharing Your Credit Card Number with Other People 61
   Paying Tax Bills with A Credit Card 62
   Applying for Credit Repair Recklessly 62
   Using Your Credit Card to Withdraw Cash 63
   Aiming for The "Rewards" 63

Ignoring Your Credit's Warning Signals 63

Chapter 7: How to Compute Your Credit Score 65

The History of Payment 65

The Amounts That You Owe 66

The Age of the Accounts 67

What Types of Open Accounts Do You Have? 68

The Number of Credit Applications 69

How Exactly Is It Calculated? 69

How to Check Your Credit Score 70

Chapter 8: Checking Your Credit Report 72

Where to Obtain Your Credit Report 72

How Often Are You Allowed a Free Copy of Your Credit Report? 72

Your 6-Step Credit Check Checklist 73

The 2 Things You Must Do If You Find Errors on Your Credit Report 75

Expert Tips 76

5 Bonus Tips 77

Chapter 9: The Right Mindset for Credit Management 79

Realization of Your Current Mindset 79

Don't Forget About Gratitude 79

Take Responsibility for Your Debt 80

Stop Seeing Debt-Free as a Solution to Your Problem 81

Your Get-out-of-Debt Mindset 82

Conclusion 85

BOOK 2 HOW TO BOOST YOUR CREDIT SCORE 87

Introduction *88*

Chapter 1:   Pay Your Debts *92*

    Planning 92

    Organizing 93

    Contact 93

    Negotiate 93

    Secured Credit Card 94

    Family 94

    Life Insurance 94

    Bank Borrowing 95

    Money Savers 95

Chapter 2:   Delete Bad Credit Legally *96*

    Tax Liens 96

    Judgments 96

    Dismiss A Judgment 97

    Bankruptcy 98

    Deletion of Negative Public Records (Judgments) 99

Chapter 3:   Write A Credit Repair Letter 609 .... *101*

    Keep All of the Records 101

    Add in the Identification Information 102

    Consider Bringing Something Up, even if it Doesn't Seem Important 102

    Do Not Contact the FTC 103

Send a Letter to Each Credit Agency 104

Mention Section 609 in the Letter 105

Mention the 30-Day Limit 105

Use One of the Templates So You Know Where to Start 106

Send a Follow-Up Letter 106

Chapter 4: **Delete Inquiries Like a Pro** *108*

Chapter 5: **Recognize and Avoid Common Errors in Your Credit Report** *112*

Most Common Credit Report Errors 112

How to Prevent Common Errors on Your Credit Report? 114

Chapter 6: **Consider Credit Piggybacking** *115*

What is Credit Piggybacking? 115

Why Piggybacking Can Be Worth It 116

Possible Disadvantages of Credit Piggybacking 117

Beware of paid piggybacking services 118

What you should know before asking for the status of an authorized user 118

Chapter 7: **Order A Free Credit Report** *121*

Be Aware of Imposters 123

Chapter 8: **Be Familiar with the Credit Bureaus** *125*

TransUnion 125

Experian 125

Equifax 126

Making the Best of Credit Bureaus 126

How the Bureaus Get Their Information 127

Chapter 9: Check If You Are a Victim of Identity Theft and How to Fix It   129

How Identity Theft Happens 129

What to Do If You're a Victim of Identity Theft 132

Protecting Yourself from Identity Theft 136

Chapter 10:   Acquire the Right Mindset 138

Avoiding the Bad Credit with the Right Mindset 138

Features of a Bad Money Mindset 138

Qualities of a Positive Money Mindset 139

Find Financial Balance 140

A Money Mantra 141

Chapter 11:   Take Advantage of the Consumer Credit Laws 142

The Fair Credit Acts 142

How The Fair Credit Acts Protect You 144

Chapter 12:   Make Sure to Do Credit Monitoring 147

What Happens with Credit Monitoring? 147

Advantages 148

Disadvantages 150

Chapter 13:   Get Rid of Your Collection Accounts Once and for All   152

Collections 152

Settling Large Collections 155

How to Handle Medical Collections 157

Will Paying My Collection Accounts Increase My Score? 158

Collections: A Step-by-Step Process 158

Chapter 14: Avoid Foreclosure at All Costs........................... *160*

What is Foreclosure? 160

The Two Types of Foreclosure 162

Stages of Foreclosure.. 163

What to Do When You Default? 164

Effects of Foreclosure on Credit Scores............................... 166

Conclusion *168*

BOOK 3 609 LETTER TEMPLATES & CREDIT REPAIR SECRETS ***171***

Introduction... *172*

Chapter 1: What is Section 609?... *176*

Section 609 176

Why Use a 609 Letter?... 178

Chapter 2: How to Open a Dispute *181*

Some Helpful Steps for Writing a Section 609 Letter 182

Some Other Things to Consider 184

Chapter 3: Tips to Have Success with 609.......................... *187*

Include Documentation 187

Be Thorough 188

Illustrate Your Case 189

Proofread the Letter Thoroughly 189

Get Advice If Necessary 189

What Not to Disclose in Your Letter 190

Make Sure Everything Is Readable 191

Do not Bypass the Credit Reporting Agency 191

Chapter 4: What Next? How to Proceed with the Letters?.. 193

    Emails 193

    Doing it All Online 194

    Telephone 195

    Mail 196

    Certified Mail 196

Chapter 5: 12 Templates of 609 Letter 199

    Letter #1: Initial Letter to Credit Bureau Disputing Items 199

    Letter #2: When You Don't Get a Response from Letter #1 201

    Letter #3: Request for Removal of Negative Items from Original Creditor 203

    Letter #4: If You Don't Receive a Response from Letter #3 205

    Letter #5: If the Credit Bureau Doesn't Remove Negative Items Disputed 207

    Letter #6: Affidavit of Unknown Inquiries 209

    Letter #7: Affidavit of Suspicious Addresses 210

    Letter #8: Affidavit of Bankruptcy 212

    Letter #9: Affidavit of Erroneous Entry 213

    Letter #10: Affidavit for Account Validation 214

    Letter #11: Affidavit of Request for Method Verification 216

    Letter #12: Affidavit for Validation 218

Chapter 6: How to Avoid Wrong Inquiries 220

Hard Inquiries 220

Soft Inquiries 222

Managing Inquiries 223

Chapter 7:   Frequently Asked Questions about Credit Score 226

Can Credit Scores Change Very Much Over Time? 226

What Are the Minimal Requirements for a Credit Score? 226

What Are the Various Types of Late Payments and How Do They Affect My Credit Score? 226

How Do I Reduce the Negative Impact of Bankruptcy? 227

Collections—How Should I Deal with Them and What Do They Do to My Credit? 227

How Do I Go About Establishing a Credit History? 227

How Do Lenders Use FICO Scores in the Context of Credit Scores? 227

How Can I Obtain a Free Credit Report and Credit Score from Each Bureau? 228

How Long Can Negative Information on My Credit Report Remain? 228

Can I Improve My FICO Score if My Only Credit Account Is a Charge Card? 228

Will Closing a Credit Card Account Boost My FICO Score? 228

What Impact Would the "Credit Squeeze" Have on Me? 228

How Can I Keep My Credit Safe if Disaster Strikes? 229

Do you have any kind of overdraft protection? 229

What Exactly Are Inquiries, and How Do They Affect My FICO Score? 229

Would Getting My Credit Reports Harm or Lower My Credit Score? 229

Does Paying My Bills to Help My Credit? 230

Would a Charge Off or a Collection Account Be Removed from My Credit Report if I Pay It Off? 230

Is Credit Repair Simple? Will Consumers Do It on Their Own? .230

Are the Credit Bureaus a Government Branch? 230

If I Successfully Delete a Negative Item from My Credit Report, Will It Reappear on My Report? 231

Is It Legal for Creditors to Exclude a Negative, Accurate Listing from My Credit Report? Is It True That Items Remain on the Credit Report for Seven Years? 231

Chapter 8: Goodwill Letters 232

Goodwill Letter Template 233

Cease and Desist Letters 234

Chapter 9: More Tips 237

Tips on Filing a Dispute with Section 609 237

The Necessary Documents before Sending the Letter 239

Where to Send Your 609 Letters? 240

Tips for Letter Writing 242

Chapter 10: How to Reach 800+ Credit Score 244

Chapter 11: Credit Repair 248

Lifestyle Changes and Financial Strategies 249

Pay Bills on Time 249

> **Pay More than the Minimum**..250
>
> **Maintain Low Credit Card Balances**...250
>
> **Pay Maxed-Out Cards First** 251
>
> *Conclusion* *252*

BOOK 1
CREDIT SCORE HACKS

Learn the Secrets That Credit Repair Agencies Won't Tell You to Boost Your FICO Score On Your Own by 200 Points in Less Than 30 Days...Written By the Owner of a Credit Agency!

Introduction

This number is gathered from credit bureaus that have created credit reports for this specific purpose. In order to create these credit reports, the credit bureaus take a look at various factors and assign them values based on how much of a risk a person is to the bureau. As an example, FICO, one of the larger credit institutions, disclosed a general make up of exactly what is factored into a credit score. It should be noted that a FICO score is not the same as a credit score but rather a FICO score is a type of credit score.

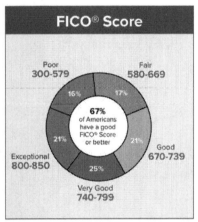 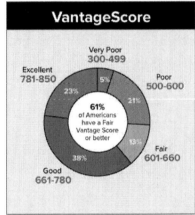

A credit score is generally composed of 10% type of credit used, 10% credit search, 15% age of credit history, 30% debt accumulation, and 35% payment history. The precise formula for a credit score is not known to the public as a rule. The components just shown are a generalization and the percentages vary with each credit institution.

Three major credit bureaus are responsible for compiling the credit information into credit reports that are then used for credit scores. These bureaus are Equifax, Experian, and TransUnion.

Each of the bureaus has grown to become established credit institutions in not just the United States, but around the world. Because of their wide reach, the information they provide is invaluable. Lenders, consumers, employers, and all manner of financial institutions use the information that the three major bureaus supply. It is with this understanding that each of the bureaus will be looked at in detail.

The first to be deliberated is TransUnion. TransUnion provides information in over 30 countries to roughly 45,000 business and 500 million consumers. TransUnion was formed in 1968 under the parent company of Union Tank Car Company and served the role of a holding company for the larger organization. In 1969, it became the owner of the Credit Bureau of Cook County and became responsible for maintaining almost 4 million card files. Later in 1981, the Marmon Group purchased TransUnion for $688 million. Goldman Sachs Capital Partners later purchased it in 2010. Four years after that TransUnion bought the data company TLO and in 2015 it became a publicly-traded company. The years of acquiring companies and becoming acquired resulted in TransUnion becoming a business that offers predictive data that determines a consumer's ability to repay loans study debt behavior.

Experian is the second of the three big bureaus used for credit scoring. It is a global company that operates in 40 countries with the corporate headquarters located in Dublin, Ireland. Formerly known as TRW Information Services, it became the bureau that it is today through a series of business deals dating back to the 1970s.

GUS plc, a retail company located in the UK, allowed for the then, novel idea, of letting customers purchase products on credit.

A computer programmer that worked for the company named John Peace combined all of the mail-order data that the various branches of GUS utilized to create a central database. The database was later expanded with electoral roll data and was commercialized in 1980 under the new name of Commercial Credit Nottingham (CCN). It was then in 1996 that GUS plc purchased Experian and merged it into the CCN. This is when Experian began to broaden its range and enter new markets around the globe before separating from GUS in 2006 to once again be its own independent entity, only now it had greater resources and capital that would lead to it becoming one of the three major bureaus.

The last of the major bureaus is Equifax. Of the three it is the oldest, having first been founded as far back as 1899. It covers information for over 88 million businesses and more than 800 million consumers. Equifax was originally founded as a Retail Credit Company based out of Atlanta, GA and rapidly grew as a company. By 1920 the company had spread throughout not just the United States but also Canada. Just a few decades later it had already grown to become one of the largest credit bureaus in America with files held on millions of citizens in North America.

The majority of Retail Credit Company's business came from creating reports for insurance companies when customers would apply for new policies. RCC was so efficient at this that the company became the main reporter for all of the major insurance companies.

The information that was investigated included more than just an individual's finances or health, but also a person's habits, morals, and other such statistics. This created controversy for the company during the 1960s and 1970s due to not just the information collected but also the company's willingness to sell the information to virtually anyone.

Some of the more controversial information collected included a person's marital troubles, school history, political activities, and even their sex life. Because of this, the US Congress had to hold a hearing when RCC attempted to computerize its records. The hearings led to the Fair Credit Reporting Act which regulated information stored about consumers by corporations. In an effort to improve the damage caused to their company image RCC changed their name to Equifax in 1975. Under the new name, the company phased out insurance reporting and focused more on credit reporting.

Together these three bureaus are the primary sources of credit reports for credit scores. Each bureau supplies its own credit report and credit score that can go on to make up an individual's entire credit history.

Originally it was called Fair, Isaac, and Company after the name's sake of the two founders. It was then changed to Fair Isaac Corporation in 2003 before finally taking the abbreviation of FICO as the official name in 2009.

While the FICO score is the most utilized score, it is not the only score available. All credit scores that are not derived from FICO are referred to as educational credit scores. An example of an education score is VantageScore. VantageScore is a relatively newer score among the credit reporting agencies. It was created in 2006 by the three major bureaus in an attempt to compete against FICO. It is jointly owned by Equifax, Experian, and TransUnion yet it is maintained and manages as an independent company called VantageScore Solutions, LLC.

Much like FICO, VantageScore's credit scoring models use data collected by the three major bureaus to predict the risk a potential consumer would pose and to determine how likely they are to default on a loan. Also, like FICO, VantageScore utilizes a three-digit scoring system that uses higher scores to indicate lower risks. Despite the surface-level similarities between FICO and VantageScore, there are some differences.

The most obvious difference is that VantageScore's design model makes it possible to be operational with all of the three bureaus' data, as opposed to FICO which has a different model for each. Another difference is that how VantageScore calculates its scores. While FICO gives generalized percentages detailing how it comes to a credit score, VantageScore does not give any percentages. Instead of a number indicating the weight a credit item carries the calculations are created thusly: payment history is indicated as being extremely influential, the type and age of credit, as well as the percentage of a credit limit that is used, are weighted as highly influential, total debt/balance is moderately influential, lastly both recent credit and available credit are weighted as less influential.

CE Score is another different score and is published by CE Analytics. It is used by such sites as Community Empower and iQualifier. While it is free for consumers to obtain the score, it is distributed to 6,500 lenders throughout the Credit Plus network.

Given the amount of information that is gathered in a credit report, it is important to know just how that information is used. A person's credit has an effect on several major financial activities that they would want to pursue. Some of the activities are obvious, others may be surprising.

Perhaps the most well-known effect of a person's credit has been the ability to get a loan from the bank. If a person has good credit, then the bank is more likely to do business with them as the credit report is an indicator of the person's ability to pay back the loan. This means that anybody looking for a loan for a home, car, or new business would have an easier time getting the bank to cooperate with them and give them a loan. On top of being more likely to receive the loan, a person with a good credit score can also expect to have a much more manageable interest rate. The bank trusts the person to make payments on time and does not expect the person to be much of a risk. The person is seen as dependable so the bank is not going to apply any pressure to ensure they are paid back.

Another obvious effect is how a person's ability to get a credit card is affected. The same rules for getting a loan from a bank apply to getting a credit card with a few differences. A person with a less-than-perfect credit score can still get a credit card, but there will be some restrictions in place. A person may only get a credit card from specific companies and with a much smaller spending limit, for example. The interest rate may also be much higher because the individual is seen as a greater risk.

The interest rate on a person's mortgage depends on the credit of the individual. The lower the score then the worst the interest is for the person.

Utilities are also affected by a person's credit. The utility companies may charge extra fees or higher rates to a person with less than perfect credit. With the higher fees attached to utilities ultimately, a person may have higher bills month to month. This means that instead of having a normal power bill, for example, the individual has to incur a greater fee that they otherwise would not have to pay if their credit was in a better standing.

Cellphone providers and insurance agencies may also do the same as the utilities, with the former having the ability to not just restrict the level of service a customer may receive but even outright turn down customers.

One of the more surprising impacts of a person's credit is on their romantic relationships. Studies have shown that those with good credit tend to have stronger relationships that last longer. An interesting fact that should be taken into consideration is that those of similar credit standings often end up having successful relationships as well. This is because similar credit standings, whether good or bad, can be seen as an indicator about their attitude towards money and finances. Simply put, those who have similar attitudes towards money are more likely to be compatible in other areas as well. However, it should not be ignored that 40% of adults are stated, according to these studies, as saying that knowing a person's credit score affects their desire to date that person.

If one person has great credit but the other doesn't then the lower credit score could prevent the couple from receiving the loan. This creates a feeling of being a burden on the person that has a lower credit score and can lead to hostilities.

Credit simply does not work in a way that would allow that to be the case. Instead, the bad credit weighs both individuals down and causes the person with good standing in their credit to incur the same penalties as the other, especially if they filed jointly for any financial endeavor. For example, if a couple were to apply for a home loan together the good credit of one individual would not boost the standing of the other's bad credit. This is because negative and positive items in credit reports are weighted differently from each other.

Chapter 1: The FICO Score

What is a FICO Score?

The credit score structure was formulated by the Fair Isaac Corporation also referred to as FICO. This credit score is utilized by financial institutions. There are other credit score models; however, the FICO score is the one that is most commonly used. Consumers can get and keep high credit scores by simply making sure their debt level remains low, and they maintain an extended history of paying their bills as and when they are due.

In the FICO scoring formula, not all credit reports are scored equally.

Credit scores are weighted based on the particular "scorecard" that a person falls under.

For example, if the person has filed for bankruptcy, they may be scored using a special "bankruptcy" scorecard.

The credit score for a person under one scorecard may be affected differently by a negative event, like a late payment, than someone with the same event on a different scorecard.

The scorecard you're on is determined by the most recent significant event in your credit history.

The first 10 scorecards go something like this...

Scorecards 1–5:

- Those with public records, including judgments and bankruptcy, on their credit report
- For those with serious delinquencies other than bankruptcies (60, 90, 120 latest, collections, judgments, charge-offs repossessions, etc.).
- Those with only 1 credit account (very thin files)
- Those with only 2 credit accounts (thin files)
- Those with 3 credit accounts only.

Scorecards 6–10 should NOT have ANY grave felonies (the definition of "serious" is unknown):

- 0–2 year's oldest account
- 2–5 year's oldest account
- 5–12 year's oldest account
- 12–19 year's oldest account
- 19+ years oldest account

There is a total of 12 scorecards, and they are subject to change as FICO (formerly Fair Isaac Corp) updates its scoring formula.

How Do You Check Your Credit Score?

This is not entirely the case. Credit reports usually do not include your credit score. It's also important to note that you do not have only one credit score. You will have at least three and more if you include the Vantage Score. They should similar in range but will not usually be the same number because they are an estimate based on a series of calculations.

There are a few different ways you can try to access your credit scores. Look to our list for suggestions:

- Check with your financial institutions. Many loaners such as credit card companies show your credit score as part of your account for free. If your creditors do not offer this, then you might be able to find the information on your online banking. Wells Fargo, for example, updates your credit score online once a month and shows how the number has changed, and what is most influencing the score.
- Just like you can order credit reports, you can also order a copy of your score from the three main credit bureaus, and FICO directly. This is a good option if your banking institution does not offer information or you are doing your yearly credit report check.
- Some people choose to use credit score services, or free credit monitoring services to keep track of their credit score. Others offer greater resources and protection that charge, but there are many free ones.

What is a Good Credit Score?

Your credit score is split into several levels but generally ranges from 300 to 850. The different credit rating levels are label as follows:

- 300 to 600: Bad Credit
- 600 to 649: Poor Credit
- 650 to 699: Fair Credit
- 700 to 749: Good Credit
- 750 + 850: Excellent Credit

The higher your credit score, the better. Better scores allow you to get credit easier, and with lower interest rates. Even when not getting credit, such as when you are renting an apartment, having a better credit rating builds trust with potential landlords.

Increasing Your Fico Credit Score

When you improve your credit score, you can save thousands of dollars later when you get offered improved rates and terms on loans, credit cards, and mortgages. This process of repairing and improving your credit score is not something that happens overnight.

While some steps don't work overnight, if you are diligent enough to work on all of them, you are bound to see a steady pace of improvement over time. This growth is, however, dependent on your making your payments when they are due and consistently paying off your debts.

Even if you know how to improve your score, there are times when unforeseen credit disasters can occur and wreck the score you worked so hard to build.

Access to Best Credit Cards

Having a good credit score is an essential factor to qualify for an opportunity to get a credit card that provides excellent cash-back reward programs, awesome advantages, low rates, and so many others. Besides paying lower interest and fees, having access to the best credit card means you can get a larger credit limit. Therefore, you can have the freedom and flexibility to make the purchases you want without the financial constraint that arises from a small credit limit.

An increase in your credit limit results in an increase in your creditworthiness over time. This shows banks and other lending institutions that you are mature enough and can handle the responsibility of having access to a large amount of credit.

Having a good credit score can help you discover cards with cash-back rates as high as 5% at different places like restaurants, grocery stores, E-commerce platforms, gas stations, and any other time your card is used.

Easy Access to Loan

Having a bad credit history will make you scared of applying for a new credit card or loan due to the fear of being turned down. Maintaining a good credit score tells a lot about your credit responsibility. When banks and lending institutions see your credit score, they can rest assured that they are not at risk and you are likely to pay back the money you are asking them to loan to you. Though this does not guarantee outright approval because other factors such as your income, debts, etc. are also considered, it just provides you with a very good chance of getting approval.

Lower Interest Rates on Loans

The interest rate that you get to pay is directly dependent on your credit score. Suppose you have a very good credit score. In that case, you might not need to consider the interest rate when applying for a credit card because you will always qualify for the best interest rates thereby paying very minimal charges on credit card loans. If you always want your interest rate to be low, you need to have a good credit score.

Easy Approval for Rental of Houses and Apartment

So many landlords and apartment owners tend to check credit scores for the same reason lenders do routinely. They fear that tenants with bad credit scores might be unable to keep up with rent payments and avoid the hassle—they avoid tenants with a high risk. Having preceding bad credit scores gives the property owner an unsettled mind that you might not be able to pay back at the stipulated time, a good credit score says otherwise.

Better Job Applications

This is not the only criteria considered by employers, however, so many employers access the credit history of various job seekers during their application processes especially when the job you're applying for requires handling money or accessing clients' sensitive financial information. The majority of employers believe that your ability to use credit responsibly makes you more likely to be a responsible employee.

Negotiating Power

You can get leverage to negotiate a lower interest rate on your student loan, new credit card, mortgage, and others if you have a good credit score. Having a credit card with a history that doesn't have an iota of problems provides you with more bargaining power, that is needed to secure the favorable terms that you need. You therefore can carefully pick the terms that will be of great advantage to your present financial circumstance.

Chapter 2: 10 Credit Repair Myths

For a large portion of credit scoring's history, by far, most of the people engaged with loaning decisions pretty much needed to think about what hurt or helped a score. Makers of scoring formulas would not like to uncover much about how the models functioned, for dread that contenders would take their thoughts or that consumers would make sense of how to beat the framework. Luckily, today we discover much increasingly about credit scoring—however, not every person has stayed aware of the latest knowledge. Mortgage intermediaries, loan officials, credit agency agents, credit guides, and the media, among others, continue to spread outdated and out and out bogus information. Following up on their terrible guidance can put your score and your accounts at critical risk.

Myth 1: Closing Credit Accounts Will Help Your Score

This one sounds sensible, particularly when a mortgage merchant discloses to you that lenders are suspicious of people who have heaps of unused credit accessible to them. All that's you, all things considered, from hurrying out and charging up a tempest? Obviously, looking at the situation objectively, what's shielded you from piling on huge balances before now? If you've been responsible for credit before, you're probably going to continue to be responsible later. That is the essential standard behind credit scoring: Its rewards practices show moderate, responsible utilization of credit after some time because those propensities are probably going to continue.

The score likewise rebuffs conduct that is not all that responsible, for example, applying for a lot of credit you don't require. Numerous people with high credit scores locate that one of only a handful hardly any detriments for them is the number of credit accounts recorded on their reports. At the point when they go to get their credit scores, they're informed that one reason their score isn't considerably higher is that they have "too many open accounts." Many mistakenly expect they can "fix" this issue by closing accounts. In any case, after you've opened the accounts, you've done the damage. You can't fix it by closing the account. You can, however, make matters more awful.

Myth 2: You Can Increase Your Score by Asking Your Credit Card Company to Lower Your Limits

This one is a minor departure from the possibility that decreasing your accessible credit by one way or another enables your score by making you appear to be less risky to lenders. By and by, it's missing the goal. Narrowing the difference between the credit you use and the credit you have accessible to you can negatively affect your score. It doesn't make a difference that you requested the decrease; the FICO formula doesn't recognize lower limits that you mentioned and lower limits forced by a creditor. All it sees is less difference between your balances and your limits, and that is not good. If that, you need to enable your score, to handle the issue from the opposite end: by paying down your debt. Expanding the gap between your balance and your credit limit positively affects your score.

Myth 3: You Need to Pay Interest to Obtain a Good Credit Score

This is the precise inverse of the past myth, and it's similarly misinformed. You don't need to carry a balance on your credit cards and pay interest to have a good score. As you've perused a few times as of now, your credit reports—and subsequently the FICO formula—make no differentiation between balances you carry month to month and balances that you pay off. Savvy consumers don't carry credit card balances under any circumstances and do not improve their scores. Presently, the facts confirm that to get the highest FICO scores, you must have both revolving accounts, for example, credit cards, and installment loans, for example, a mortgage or car loan. What's more, except for those 0 percent rates used to drive auto deals after Sept. 11, most installment loans require paying interest.

Yet, here's a news streak: You don't have to have the highest score to get good credit. Any score more than 720 or so will get you the best rates and terms with numerous lenders. A few, particularly auto and home value lenders, save their best bargains for those with scores more than 760. You mustn't have an 850, or even an 800 score, to get incredible arrangements. In case you're attempting to improve a fair score, a little, reasonable installment loan can help—if you can get affirmed for it and pay it off on time. However, in some way or another, there's no motivation to stray into the red and pay interest.

Myth 4: Your Closed Accounts Should Indicate "Closed by Consumer," Or They Will Hurt Your Score

The hypothesis behind this myth is that lenders will see a closed account on your credit report and, if not educated generally, will accept that a nauseated creditor cut you off because you botched in some way or another. Obviously, as you most likely are aware at this point, numerous lenders never observe your real report. They're simply taking a gander at your credit score, which couldn't care less who closed a credit card. Fair Isaac figures that if a lender closes your account, it's either for dormancy or because you defaulted. If that you defaulted, that will be sufficiently archived in the account's history. If it makes you feel better to contact the bureaus and guarantee that accounts you closed are recorded as "closed by consumer," by all methods do as such. However, it won't make any distinction to your credit score.

Myth 5: Credit Counselling Is Way Worse Than Bankruptcy

Sometimes this is expressed as "credit advising is as awful as bankruptcy" or "credit directing is as terrible as a bankruptcy." None of these statements is valid. A bankruptcy recording is the single most noticeably terrible thing you can do to your credit score. On the other hand, the current FICO formula totally ignores any reference to credit guiding that may be on your credit report. Credit guiding is treated as an impartial factor, neither aiding nor hurting your score. Credit guides, if you're inexperienced with the term, have practical experience in arranging lower interest rates and also working out payment plans for debtors that may some way or another file for bankruptcy. Although credit advisors may consolidate the consumer's bills into one monthly payment, they don't give loans—as debt consolidators do—or guarantee to wipe out or settle debts for not exactly the chief amount you owe.

The fact that credit guiding itself won't affect your score doesn't mean, notwithstanding, that enrolling in a credit advisor's debt management plan will leave your credit sound. A few lenders will report you as late only for enrolling in a debt management plan. Their thinking is that you're not paying them what you initially owed, so you ought to need to endure some agony. Not all credit instructors are made equivalent, and some have been blamed for retaining consumer payments that were proposed for creditors.

Myth 6: Pre-Employment Screens Use Credit Scores

This is a common issue that worries all. Some people have bad credit, and they need to get a job to work on it. Then they're told that they won't be ready to get jobs because their credit score is just too low. However, credit scores aren't and have never been used by employers for job-related purposes.

However, credit reports, which are a little different from credit scores, are often used for employment screening purposes, but that only happens if you allow them access.

Spreading out your balances on credit cards through a single card can harm your credit scores. Remember that tons of the models, including the FICO and Vantage Score, will work with tons of things to calculate these overall scores. The second most important metric is debt load or the quantity and sort of debt.

The fewer accounts you have with a balance, the higher is your credit score. If you've got a MasterCard that doesn't carry a balance, it will impact your credit score positively. It is often because those cards will have a debt to limit the ratio of 0 percent.

Myth 7: The Worth of Your Account Age Will Be Lost When a Card Is Closed

Closing a MasterCard account won't result in losing out on the worth of how long you had that card. Credit scoring models are still going to consider the age of accounts that have been closed once they find out your credit score for as long as that's still on your credit report. A number of these will still age once they are closed.

It is possible that closing this card will impact the score because it takes away the quantity of credit that you have. It is often even worse because it messes with some ratios if you continue to balance those out, but it's not going to mess with the age of the account.

Credit scores will reward customers who don't have tons of debt, and people who have zero MasterCard debt will be awarded the most. The assumption that you need to carry tons of debt to possess good scores is a false idea and is practiced by those who do not understand these scores.

Myth 8: Once You Ruin Your Credit, You'll Never Rebuild It

A credit report is more of a history of your credit, and if you give it enough time, credit is something that could be rebuilt. It generally shows us how things are right at a particular point in time and keeps an extended record of all the credit that the individual consumer will open up in their name. It will show us the inactive and closed accounts, but the history is retained irrespective of anything.

Late or missed payments can often reflect in a report for up to seven years in many cases. But it's still possible to go through and rebuild credit. You've got to take the time to pay all of your debts on time, search for some better options for credit, and learn more about how credit and money works. Additionally, the longer the credit history can maintain limited negative information, the higher it is. If you do have some negatives on your credit score, the older it is, the smaller it becomes.

Myth 9: Checking Your Report Will Harm Your Score

If a consumer takes the time to access their report, it's not going to affect their score in the least. You may take a glance at your credit report as often as you wish to confirm that it's accurate, up-to-date, and there's no missing information.

When someone applies for credit, though, the lender takes out the applicant's credit report, which may end up being a tough inquiry. The report may be shown to another lender who wants to look at your report because they will show new debt that doesn't yet show abreast of the credit report. These will affect our credit scores. Suppose you have too many of those on a report. In that case, it means that you are applying for too much credit directly or that you are being rejected for a few reasons, which is a bad sign.

Myth 10: Bankruptcy Protection Will Be Excellent for Those Who Have Large Amounts of Debt

We have to understand that bankruptcy is a legal process that will relieve an individual from paying their debts. Depending on the sort of bankruptcy, a person could also be in a situation where he/she is unable to pay off any of the debt, and at other times they'll be willing to repay a part of it.

However, this is not a get-free card. It will be something that shows abreast of your report for ten years in some cases and may make it almost impossible for you to get credit. Consumers should only opt for it if they're absolutely out of options, and they must consider working with a credit counselor as it will give them a better shot at repaying the debts and keep things in check. In some cases, one can even settle the debts for fewer than the first amount to save credit once he/she gets into trouble.

Chapter 3: What is Bad for Credit Score

Good credit is critical to achieving your financial goals and can impact your life in ways you may not be aware of. We'll go over what's bad for your score. These six behaviors are all ways that you could be hurting yourself and potentially preventing yourself from borrowing money.

Multiple Inquiries

The inquiry sits on your report for two years unless it is reported on more than one bureau, in which case it stays on the report essentially forever. The purpose of this inquiry is to help make sure you are not a fraud and are eligible for the credit or loan that has been requested.

Example of what can happen if you have multiple inquiries:

You ask for a $10,000 loan at 6 percent interest. The processing company says that is great, but they need another hard inquiry on your report. They will run three separate inquiries against all three credit bureaus. That gives you a hard inquiry for each bureau every 365 days; one year from now it will still be there even after all three bureaus have reported it. It will never drop off.

The higher the number of inquiries, the riskier it looks, and may adversely hurt your credit score. Keep that in mind before applying for multiple loans at once. A good rule of thumb is to have no more than 10 inquiries per year.

Being Over-Extended

Being over-extended is having too much debt in comparison with income and assets (or having too little income concerning expenses). Most people who work on their credit report realize that having too much debt is bad, but what they may not know is the effect that having a large amount of debt has on your score.

To figure out how much debt you have compared with income, the credit bureaus take your total monthly obligations (divided by 12) and add them to your monthly income. If this number is less than $350, it is considered normal and good for your credit score. If this number is $350 to $500, it's considered borderline and will have a limited negative effect on your score; if it's more than $500 it will start causing serious damage to your overall credit score.

The average credit score in the United States is about 700. If we use $350 of income to debt ratio, a $500 to $700 credit-to-debt ratio is borderline and a higher credit-to-debt ratio would be considered overextended.

Too Many Cards Applications

After you apply for a card, the bank will run a hard inquiry on your report; when you apply for two or more cards at once, it is called Multiple Hard Inquiries (or MHI). This will lower your score for some time; in some rare cases, it can even drop you by as many as 100 points. The best thing to do is to be very careful about the number of cards you apply for at once.

Cancelling Cards

Closing accounts can also adversely affect your credit score. You must have a good reason for closing an account and it should be done carefully.

Late Payment Loans

If you are late on a loan payment, the account will report as late-on-time on the credit bureau. Even if you are just a few days late, this fact will be reported and can hurt your score.

Non-Paying Bill/Mortgage Payment Loans

If you are not making payments for more than 60 days for a mortgage or 90 days for most other loans, then these accounts will be reported as delinquent by your bank or lender.

When you keep these simple rules in mind when applying for loans, the negative effects these habits can cause will be minimized if not completely eliminated.

These six bad credit behaviors may seem small, but when you combine them into one massive cycle of debt, you are really doing something big to your credit score. We hope this has helped you understand what is bad for your credit score and how to avoid those bad habits so that the average person can have an excellent credit profile and be able to use credit regularly.

Chapter 4: 6 Steps to Repair Bad Credit Score

If you have trouble paying your bills on time, it can have a big impact on your credit score. But with a few simple steps, you can repair that damage and get back on the financial track.

Here are six steps that will help you raise your credit score:

Step 1: Review Your Credit Score Regularly

Once every 4 months is usually enough. If something has changed, don't just blindly trust what they say! Find out for yourself what's going on and take action if necessary. Keeping tabs on this is an easy first step to fixing it (but only if the problem is not too severe).

Reviewing your credit score will give you an idea of what sort of changes might really help.

Step 2: Pay All Your Bills on Time

Late payments are the most powerful potential hit to your score. Payments reported late can do so much damage that anything else you do will not help so much. I'd suggest making it a habit to check your statement online at least once per month if it's available, or every week if not. If you think there's any chance of you getting behind, call or email that creditor and discuss your plan for paying it back. If you think something will get in the way of paying on time, make sure to let them know in advance—explain why (like "my paycheck will be late this month").

This is the single most important factor in your credit score. If you always pay your bills on time, you're not going to have a problem in this area.

You might think that if you've missed a payment or two, it's already too late to fix it. But if you catch the mistake before the credit agencies do, you can get back on track very quickly.

If not, there are still some things that will help your score more than missing out on one or two payments will hurt it.

Payment History amounts to 35% of your FICO score (remember, the higher the better).

Amounts owed are another crucial factor in your score (20%), and it doesn't matter whether you owe $3 or $300,000. If you pay off the old debt with the new one, the FICO formula will count it equally.

So, if there's a new mortgage, car loan, or line of credit that you just took out for whatever reason, don't just pay the minimum monthly payment that is required. Do whatever you can to pay it off totally within 6 months to make sure your credit score does not suffer in this area!

Avoid late payments on overdue bills unless there's an emergency (life-threatening illness). If you can't avoid it, talk to the debt collection agency or the billing company about the situation, see if they are willing to offer any leniency.

Note that every payment you make will be based on some amount of interest that is due. If you can pay off your debts in full before any interest accrues, your credit score will not be affected by this factor (which makes up 30% of your FICO score).

But some people may need to pay off their debts on time while still paying off the principle on them over time. For these people, this means keeping an eye out for situations where large amounts of their own money are being tied up.

If you have a credit card and want to transfer the balance to a 0% interest card, try transferring in smaller amounts over time, not all at once.

Try to do this ahead of time, if possible, before any late payments. Otherwise, you risk getting another late payment if you can't afford that new debt right away, or perhaps your new creditor will report that late payment. In either case, your credit score will be adversely affected by this factor (which makes up 10% of your FICO score).

Step 3: Do Not Apply for a Loan Ever Again!

Never apply for a new credit card ever again... period. In fact, find out if you have any other credit cards that you can cancel or close to prevent anyone from getting hold of them.

A lot of people don't want to report their credit cards as being closed by the companies when in fact they're not, because they're afraid that this will hurt their scores. Don't be fooled by this! This will not affect your score.

But if you tell the companies that you're done with them and they won't report the account as closed, there's a good chance that this will hurt your credit history. In other words, if you "close" a credit card after it's been reported as being active to the credit bureaus, this is going to hurt your credit score.

In some cases, people close their accounts even though they never use them because they're afraid that the account will be reported as Total Open Lines (TOL). Even if you don't use it very often, if you have an active open line of credit on your credit report it can negatively impact your score. So, if you don't use your credit cards that often, consider closing all of them and then don't apply for any new ones. By the way, this is not the same thing as applying for a new line of credit

Of course, this won't make a difference if you already have outstanding revolving debt like credit cards or something. The advice here is to close all other lines and not open any others. Every time you pay off your debts will reduce your TOL amount.

Step 4: Get Loans from Banks, Not Credit Unions

If you've read this far, chances are that you've already decided to follow all these steps—but if not, you're probably wondering whether taking out new loans through banks will affect your credit score. Which is why I'll repeat this one more time: always try to take out loans from banks instead of credit unions or small third-party lenders.

The reason is quite simple: both of them use FICO scores to decide whether or not people are approved for a loan. Credit unions only have the FICO template to use for this—it doesn't matter what type of loan you apply for because they won't do any further analysis on the information they collect.

But with banks (and other lenders like credit card companies), they will do their own independent analysis on your income, credit history, and other factors to determine whether or not you're a good candidate for a loan.

Of course, this isn't done in a malicious way. Lenders don't want to take chances with their money—and in fact, they've invested lots of time and money into educating themselves on these matters. As such, they can see that if you cannot afford to pay off your current debts, then it doesn't make any sense for them to try to give you more debt.

This is why banks want current paystubs and tax returns from prospective clients before they even consider approving them for a loan. Doing it this way ensures that the interest rate will be kept to a minimum, and it reduces the risk to the bank.

So, if you can't afford it right now, don't put yourself in a position where the lender will have to shut you down because you are unable to pay them back. If possible, get current pay stubs to provide evidence of your income.

Step 5: Use Your Credit Cards Wisely

This one can be a bit of a hassle, but you must use your credit cards effectively to get the best results.

For instance, you can buy something on your credit cards and pay off the full amount over time. Or you can only pay half the balance at the end of every month, with payments on both ends of the month. You can also combine all your cards into one MasterCard or Visa account to make it easier for you to track your spending.

Also, remember that you CANNOT put too much money on any card whether it's a debit card or a credit card. This means that even if you have a huge amount of credit available to you, that does not mean that you can apply for more credit cards. Remember that if you have too many accounts open with the same type of company, it will lower your credit score.

And this is why I mentioned earlier about using rewards cards—it's okay to use these cards to make purchases only when you are in the United States or Canada, especially if your credit limit is low.

Step 6: If You Can't Pay Off Your Debt, Pay It Off!

If you've gotten along fine with paying the minimum amount on your debts for years now, then maybe all this isn't even necessary after all. But if you've got a lot of debts, chances are that something is missing in your budget. So, get your budget under control so you can get back to paying off your debts on time each month.

But if you've got a lot of debt, it doesn't matter if you make minimum payments or not because sooner or later it will catch up to you. It's guaranteed that your credit score will be negatively affected, but just ignore this fact for now. Instead, focus on the steps above which are designed to ensure that your credit history stays clean.

But if you don't have enough money to pay off all your debts right now, then simply don't go into too much debt every month. If you can pay off your debts slowly over time, there's no reason why it shouldn't work out fine.

This is why you need to consider getting secured credit cards—you will be able to get low-interest credit if your credit isn't that great. Pay off your debt with the help of these secured credit cards if you have to, so you can get back on track. But remember: there's no point in applying for a lot of these cards in an attempt to improve your credit score because if you do, they will all show up on your report and it will be even worse for you in the long run.

To Sum Things Up

You don't need fancy tricks to improve your credit score. All you need to do is focus on the basics and use common sense when dealing with money.

If you can't afford to pay off your debts in full every month, then try to at least pay the minimum amount on time. This will help your credit score, but if things get bad with your finances in the future you might need to do more than just paying the minimum each month in order to get back on track.

And if you've got a lot of debt in the long run—big surprise there—then you really should pursue solutions that would allow you to settle all of your debts at once with only one payment every month. If that is not possible, then try seeing what possibilities are available for saving money each month so that you can make payments on all your debts soon after.

Chapter 5: The 10 Secrets the Experts Don't Share

When it comes to credit scores, I've shown you the factors that weigh the most in determining your score.

Credit scores are generated from complex mathematical formulas and algorithms that weigh and measure these factors against each other.

We can manage our behaviors to raise our credit scores outside of monitoring and keeping our credit reports error-free.

Here are ways to improve your credit scores without resorting to debt management or credit repair services.

1. Pay Bills on Time

The single-handed easiest and fastest way to boost your credit scores is to pay your bills on time.

Remember, late bill payments ding higher scores more than lower scores, so it's harder to build an excellent score back once it's hit with late payment.

Also, remember that late payments are logged on credit reports only after they are 30 days past due, so you can relax if you missed your payment by a couple of days. Don't get into this habit, however, because late payments on credit cards may translate into higher finance charges overall.

Creditors always note in the fine print that once late payments are logged, your APRs may go up, so be very careful about paying your bills on time.

2. Challenge Late Fees

As eager as they are to hit you with late fees and higher finance charges, creditors can also be somewhat forgiving if you call in to request a late fee to be waived.

Just like the ball is in your court to maintain an accurate credit record, it's your responsibility to dispute late fees.

I've been successful at having late fees removed when I've requested this from creditors, and my paying my bills on time probably helps with these requests.

Explain that you missed your payment because you were on vacation, or that you simply forgot this one time (if you are a timely-paying customer, stress this point), and the creditor will likely waive your late fee.

3. Set Up Payment Alerts

Technology now assists in so many ways by reminding you of bill payments when due.

Also, not receiving a monthly paper statement does not mean you can skip that payment. Your agreement with the creditor is that you will repay your debt or the minimum amount due by the due date, so try to get it in on time.

Set up e-mail or text payment reminders. Auto-schedule your bill payments. If you have a mobile app for your creditor, allow a push notification on the payment date.

4. Keep Your Older Accounts Open

If you've got older credit cards with high credit lines, keep those accounts open. The older, the better. The smaller the amount charged against the maximum allowed, the better.

The length of your overall credit history accounts for 15 percent of your credit score, so keeping your older accounts open is a good idea.

This also helps your overall credit utilization rate, the second-highest contributing factor to your credit score.

If you are desperate to decrease the number of credit cards you have, only close out merchant cards, such as retail cards that were offered at the time you were buying something—if you know you're unlikely to use them again.

Add to this any cards with small available credit lines that you're probably not going to use again—the older cards with the higher credit limits matter more.

5. Forget About Older Derogatory Accounts

The more recent a negative item, the more damage it is doing to your credit score. As negative items age, they have less of an impact on a credit score.

Years ago, it was ill-advised to pay off older collections beyond three years old because payment would then log a more recent reporting date and bring the collection back from the dead, ultimately hurting your credit scores.

While the CRAs will say that they have improved this conundrum by working with collection agencies, I simply wouldn't take the risk.

Some have referred to this as the creditor "dusty pile" or simply put, "letting sleeping dogs lie."

It is also a bad idea to pick up the phone and call on collection agencies regarding your old collections.

Collection agencies, through a tactic called "re-aging", will sometimes bring a file back from the dead and restart the statute clock once any new activity has been received, including offers to settle.

While this is illegal, don't initiate it—imagine how delighted the collection agency would be to dust off your file when it has already assumed it won't receive anything for the debt.

6. Stop Buying Things on Credit

If you've got a spending problem, then it's time to rein in the expenses.

I've resorted to some pretty extreme measures to avoid spending on credit which include leaving the credit cards at home (which means I can't splurge), cutting up credit cards (which means I can't use physically use them), and unlinking them from smartphone wallet apps (which means I must pay in cash or by debit card).

7. Mind Your Balances

Pay your balances in full monthly, or keep them low. Remember that 15 percent of a credit score was due to the total credit utilized, or the amount owed versus the amount of total available credit.

How much debt you carry month to month on your unsecured debt—debt on credit cards—has a significant impact on your credit score.

If you can keep these balances as low as possible, preferably under 30 percent of your total credit, then your credit score will be healthier than if you were being close to maxed out. For example, if you have a $10,000 credit limit, then it's ideal to not carry a balance of more than $3,000 from statement to statement.

I realize that for those who currently have high credit card debt, this may not be feasible, at least not for a while.

But you can chip away at your debt slowly, paying over and above your monthly finance charges to get your balances down.

Carrying very small balances on your credit cards from month to month, as long as you pay the amount due by the due date won't hurt. I'm talking about carrying less than 5 percent of the total balance, not leaving your balances close to maxed out, if you can help it. Monthly credit usage stimulates reporting and history and also shows credit management.

Ideally, paying off the full amounts charged every month will save you the most money from high credit card finance charges anywhere in the range of the 14 to 20 percent mark, and you'll be helping out your credit score a great deal.

8. Pay Down Your Debt at Lower Costs

Another option could be to consolidate unsecured debt with a fixed loan at a lower APR.

Your goal here is to not shift debt around but to actually make a dent in it.

If you have high credit card debt, consider consolidating your high-interest debt with credit cards offering zero interest fees for transferred balances, and zero interest on new purchases for some time.

While I wouldn't normally recommend the shifting around of debt, taking advantage of credit offers with introductory zero percent APR periods (the longer the better) can provide an opportunity for your payments will have a more significant impact on balance reduction.

9. Mix Up Your Credit

Manage your mix of unsecured (considered bad if you carry high balances) and secured debt (better because it's tied to assets).

If you've got a couple of credit cards, an auto loan, and a student loan, then that's a pretty diverse mix. Utilize the cards by charging small balances and paying them in full monthly and continue paying timely on those installment loans.

Credit scoring favors good credit usage and behaviors, so you'll want to keep your accounts open and paid timely.

Some people make the mistake of not using their credit cards at all; however, if you carry little to no credit card debt, resume small amounts of charging activity to boost your score. Just remember to pay all bills on time.

10. Limit New Credit Applications

Don't obtain new credit unless you absolutely must do so.

Each new credit card application counts as a hard pull, which hurts your credit. It also results in brand new credit being logged, which re-ages your overall combined length of credit history.

Just say "No thanks," the next time you're asked if you'd like to open a new credit account because "it will save you x percentage on your total purchases for that day."

Ask yourself, "Do I really need to open this card?"

If you had intended to pay cash, then do so. Or use an existing credit card, and pay your purchases off timely. Opening new merchant accounts not only tempts you to spend more but also runs the risk of leaving credit balances longer and subject to interest fees.

Note: Do Not Forget to Monitor Credit Activity

Many companies these days offer some type of credit monitoring service that will alert you in case of any new credit activity. These services are a great first recourse to discovering any outside attempts at identity theft or fraud.

Hard inquiries for new credit applications generally raise the biggest flags, since these imply that new credit has been requested. If you didn't make the request, then you should investigate the origin of the inquiry and the creditor.

For credit monitoring, I've used Lifelock for years. The company charges a monthly fee to alert consumers by e-mail or phone whenever a new credit application is detected.

Credit Sesame's monitoring service also offers an extensive geolocating social security activity tracker, which can alert you as to the area where your SSN has been used for credit applications.

The three CRAs also offer monitoring, but I think that the third-party service providers do it comprehensively and with better data and technology.

In recent identity theft cases, thieves targeted the valid social security numbers of toddlers and newborn babies for credit card and loan applications.

All the more reason to be vigilant about how and to whom you disclose you and your family's social security numbers.

Any sensitive paper documentation leaving your household should always be crosscut shredded and disposed of properly.

Chapter 6: Mistakes You Should Avoid When Dealing with Your Credit Score

For many people, a credit card is merely a convenient way to make transactions. However, few people realize that the little plastic card also has the ability to wreak havoc on their lives if not used carefully. Ultimately, misusing your credit account can destroy your credit scores and ultimately hamper your credit.

One way to prevent the damages that poorly handled credit can cause is to know about the mistakes that people commonly make and learn how to avoid them.

Paying Just the Minimum

Issuers of credit cards set a minimum amount that you should pay every billing period. Some people have the wrong notion that this is a godsend because it is so small compared to the total amount. They couldn't be more wrong.

To avoid having to pay more in the long run, try to pay the total balance every billing cycle. Don't let it accrue interest.

Ignoring Your Billing Statement

If you don't check your credit card's billing statement often, the more likely it is that you'll risk missing a payment or paying less than you should have for it to be considered on time.

In addition, ignoring your card's statement will cause you to miss some important announcements, such as an announcement of the changes on your credit card's terms.

Make it a habit to check your billing statement because it will often be your guide to know if there are any false activities on your account. Besides, doing so will help you keep your spending in check.

Canceling Your Credit Card

Now that you have finally paid off all your credit card bills which have been stressing you out for ages, your first impulse might be to get rid of your credit card as soon as possible, which is usually done by cutting up your card and closing your account.

But don't be too quick on doing that, as closing down your account so suddenly can actually lower your credit score. Keep in mind that the age of your accounts affects your credit scores.

Even if you have paid off your credit card, it would be much better for you if you just leave your credit account open, that is until you are 100% sure that you can offset the possible reduction in credit score by making changes that would boost it. Just keep it open and maintain low utilization.

Paying Late

Always pay for your monthly payments on time. If you keep on forgetting about your due dates, then you should come up with a system that can remind you about them. For example, you can set up auto-pay with your bank or use apps to set reminders. If the primary reason is an inconvenience, then organize your bills so you could schedule the best time to pay all if not most of them.

If you keep on paying late for your monthly payments, it can cost you up to $38 in late fees, which will also depend on the number of times you have been late for the past 6 months.

Also, falling behind your payments for more than 30 days will also affect your credit score. But if your existing payment is more than 60 days late, then your card's issuer may raise your interest rate up to the penalty rate available.

Loaning Your Credit Card

When you loan your credit card to another person, you will no longer have control over the purchases that they are about to make.

In the end, you'll still be responsible for paying all the bills, even if the person who borrowed your card doesn't pay you for the expenses.

Never ever loan your card to someone, even if it's someone you know, except if you are prepared to take responsibility to pay for the purchases that they are about to make.

Not Knowing Your Credit Card Terms

If you know how your credit card company handles late payments, you'll be more likely to pay your card's bill on time. After all, you'll know exactly how much they cost you.

Letting Your Card Get Charged-Off

Acquiring a charge-off is one of the worst things that can happen to your credit card report and credit score.

It would take about a total of 6 months of missed payments for you to be charged with a charge-off status. Before your card gets to that point, ensure your delinquent accounts are current.

Applying for Too Much Credit

If you are on the checkout line and the cashier asked if you want to apply for a store credit card for the discount, do not accept it outright.

You may love to have a discount on your purchases, but it is still a credit card. Remember that each time you apply for credit, an inquiry will show up on your credit report and will pull down your credit score a little. The discount you think you'll be getting might not be worth it.

Also, be careful about opening too many credit accounts if you plan on applying for big loans, such as a mortgage, car loan, and others.

Maxing Your Card Out

Utilizing more than 30% of your card's limit can be quite dangerous for your credit score. Also, getting close to your credit limit will put you at risk for fees that are over the limit, and even the penalty interest will increase your card's charges once you exceed your credit card's limit.

Therefore, to have a manageable payment amount and healthy credit score, always maintain a good credit card balance.

Getting Pressured into Accepting New Cards

Have you ever noticed that sometimes most of the letters in your mail are about new credit card offers? Or maybe you have encountered countless strangers who are calling you to pitch you one? Well, don't think that these are just your imagination, because they are not.

A lot of credit card companies send out millions or even billions of credit offers every year, but this doesn't mean that you have to accept all of their requests or listen to their sale pitches. You can freely choose to get out of the prescribed credit card offers and out of the credit card telemarketing lists.

You can also get out of the email and phone solicitations from the mortgage companies.

Sharing Your Credit Card Number with Other People

Some credit card holders sometimes share their card numbers to pay for a bill. But if someone calls, emails, or have mailed you with some requests and unsolicited personal information, such as your Social Security number or credit card number, never reveal it even if the person sounds legitimate or nice. These kinds of requests are part of financial scams that mostly target seniors. These fraudsters are trying to make unauthorized use of your good name and credit or steal your money.

If you do become a victim of identity theft, immediately report it to your Federal Trade Commission and to your local police department.

Paying Tax Bills with A Credit Card

If you don't pay for a federal tax debt, the IRS will have the power to tax your assets, put a right to claim or hold your property, or seize your tax refunds. However, none of it should intimidate you into paying them with your credit card.

The reason is that if you use your credit card, you will also have to pay an interchange fee. This may run anywhere from 2% to 4% of the amount that you are paying for.

Now, add those to the 12% to 18% interest that you have to pay to your bank if you think of adding the tax charge to your balance. A better solution to your problem would be to set up a repayment plan with the IRS and pay your tax debts over time.

Applying for Credit Repair Recklessly

If you have recently gone through a serious personal setback such as a foreclosure, divorce, or bankruptcy, your credit standing might be shaky or maybe even downright bad.

However, looking for a quick fix can actually put you in the hands of a con artist that specializes in tricking people i.e., charge you with hidden costs or high upfront fees for their fake services.

Also, be aware of companies or an individual that promises to "fix" your bad credit overnight. Fixing a really bad credit score won't happen overnight, it lasts for days, weeks, or maybe even a month if the process is slow.

Using Your Credit Card to Withdraw Cash

Using credit cards to withdraw cash could be bad because the credit card issuer is not able to monitor the spending, and thus view it as a high-risk loan and subsequently charge higher interests.

If you don't fully pay off the amount you withdrew within a month, your balance will start racking up some interests. Therefore, you can quickly lose control over your debt if not handled as soon as possible, particularly if you only pay the minimum amount monthly.

Aiming for The "Rewards"

We people have been known to use credit for all kinds of things, be it a lavish vacation or jewelry, or even cars and in some cases, expensive novelty products.

However, making large purchases on a credit card is definitely a no-no unless you are 100% sure that you can immediately pay off such large amounts in full.

Whatever benefits that you may gain, in terms of flier miles or hotel check-ins, will come with interest charges, which you'll have to pay if you don't immediately pay your balance off every month.

Ignoring Your Credit's Warning Signals

To improve your chances of getting a healthy credit rating, check your credit reports for free at least once or twice a year from a government-mandated website. However, if you're in the process of building or rebuilding credit, that isn't just enough. Check it once a month. You may also want to sign up for credit monitoring services, among others.

Also take note of warning signs that indicate you might be in debt trouble such as missing payments, only making minimum payments, regularly seeking for 0% card offers, a low-rate balance transfers just to afford payments, or charging without knowing how to pay for bills.

If any of the following warning signals are familiar to you, it's time you get your act together to start repairing your credit.

Chapter 7: How to Compute Your Credit Score

The credit score is calculated using several pieces of your credit report. If you want to have a high credit score or have good credit, you must know how it is calculated and what factors (banks and credit agencies) to take into account to approve or deny a loan or credit card.

Your credit score is calculated based on these categories, namely:

- The history of Payment
- The amounts that you owe
- The age of the accounts
- What types of open accounts do you have?
- The number of credit applications

Let's examine these factors and see how we can raise your credit score one by one.

The History of Payment

Consider making payments on or even earlier than the agreed time as it is absolutely important and has a major impact on your score. If you make late payments, then your credit score will dramatically reduce.

The fundamental thing a lender would want to find out is whether or not you paid your bills or even your credit loans in a good time. This category out of the others majorly influences your credit score and makes up to 35% of your score, which is why it is very important to take note of it.

Now that you know that delayed payments can affect your credit score and also hinder you from building a good credit history, you must do well to ensure you pay all debts on time without any qualms.

The types of accounts normally considered for payment history are namely:

- Installment Loans
- Credit Cards (such as Visa, Master Card, and so on)
- Loans to the consumer
- Retail accounts and;
- Mortgage Loans

Remember, the path of making and building a good credit score is a path that will require you to make payments on time.

The Amounts That You Owe

It is no coincidence that the amounts that you owe are the next thing to talk about. This is because, after the history of payment, it is known to be the next most influencing factor of your credit score.

It is already a general rule that you are required to use only 30% of the credit the bank approves to you and nothing more than that. It will be highly unwise if you go ahead to use all the credit that the bank approves, say $300 on a $1000 credit card. That means you should never make use of the maximum account that has been allowed on your card.

Credit bureaus perceive this as an omen when you start to depend on the money and they tend to withdraw as it signifies a negative mark for your credit report and also your credit score.

I would advise you to use below 30% of your credit, or what's best is you could go-ahead to use only 10% of your credit line and nothing more than that. By doing this, you will have better credit scores and your chances of increasing and even sustaining a good credit score will be limitless.

The amount of money that you owe is also a key factor to consider when calculating your score.

The Age of the Accounts

Consistency is key in the credit score world. As long as you keep maintaining a good credit score history, your credit score will always remain high. The general rule explains as the longer you have credit cards, the more your credit score increases. That's why I'll advise you to start your credit as soon as you can. This is a factor that constitutes about 15% of your credit score, measuring the length at which you have your credit accounts and how well you have been able to manage them within that period.

Here are what your FICO credit score records:

- It takes into account the age of both the new and old accounts and even the average age of all of your accounts.
- It also takes into account your credit lines (if you have), how long you have been with them, and how your payment history has been.
- And finally, it measures the exact age of your loans/credit cards. Because of this, many professionals advise that older

accounts should neither be closed nor canceled as it is likely to affect your credit score.

There's a high possibility of you having a high credit score by having a long time with your credit.

What Types of Open Accounts Do You Have?

Another factor that can favor your credit score is having various types of loans (mortgages, cars, and student loans) and credit cards.

Your credit score is majorly concerned with the different types of credit that you use, some of which exist are credit cards, mortgage loans, installment loans, and accounts with finance companies too.

Do take note that it is not so important that you use each one of them and I'll advise that you only open accounts that you really are going to use.

The credit mix has no major effect on your credit score, but it is of great importance that your credit report does not contain excess information on which your score is based.

As it were, there is really no perfect version of a credit mix as it varies with time from individual to individual. Opening car loans, student loans, and credit cards you won't be needing won't be advisable for you.

Although, it would be an added advantage to have this factor that shows that you know how to handle your credit responsibly.

The Number of Credit Applications

Lastly, the quantity of applications to your credit to some extent distresses your credit score. Every time you apply for a loan or possibly a credit card (even if not yet approved), your credit score slightly decreases.

Opening various credit accounts within a very short time can be very risky for financial institutions, most especially when it's a case of one who does not have a lengthy credit history. This explains why many people see that their credit score has decreased either when they open a credit card or are approved for a particular loan. However, the decline is temporary.

Also, bear in mind that credit checks vary. Interestingly, checking your credit will have your credit score reduced if and only if it is a hard inquiry. There are hard inquiry and soft inquiry of which I will explain below.

A hard inquiry is made when a loan is applied to a lender. That may include a student loan, car, mortgage loan. These inquiries affect your credit score.

While the soft inquiry is made when you request a copy of your credit report, apply for a job or maybe use it for a credit monitoring service. These types of inquiries in no way affect your credit score.

How Exactly Is It Calculated?

As important as it is to calculate your credit score, it is also very important to know that these factors have no fixed percentage as they may vary due to the financial information obtained from your credit report.

This goes to say that without adequate knowledge of the basic factors above, there is a tendency for an individual to be careless in the decisions he makes at obtaining a high credit score. It is hence very important that these factors are known.

Though these factors are applied when calculating a credit report, the level of importance varies from person to person.

It is not possible to record the impact of each of the factors on the credit score without acknowledging the report as a whole.

How to Check Your Credit Score

Some services enable you to check your credit score at very little or no cost. However, you must take caution and use services that you know are reliable, so you don't fall into the hands of scammers on the Internet. Some of these reliable services, especially the ones listed below, have no cost.

Some of these services are:

- Experian: This US credit agency is used by several lenders to evaluate your credit and requires you to pay just $1 to view your credit.
- TransUnion: This credit bureau also allows you to see your score quickly and easily. It is also used by lenders as well as banks to estimate your credit.
- Quizzle: This is a credit score simulator that offers a Vantage Score that is based on TransUnion data.
- Mint: This is another simulator that utilizes data from the Equifax credit agency.

Credit cards that allow you to see your credit score

It is also very possible to obtain your credit score for FREE by having some particular credit cards at your disposal. Asides from the bonus rewards you get, these cards improve the quality of your credit score and notify you immediately there is any form of suspicious activity. Here are two that I can guarantee are simply the best.

Discover IT credit card

Discover IT credit card is known to be one of the best credit cards of recent. This card uses Experian data to display your credit score monthly.

Monthly, your credit tracker is updated, notifying you of sudden changes in your credit report. Also, it is accepted internationally and is relatively easy to obtain.

CreditWise from Capital One

The Capital One credit card features the CreditWise credit simulator, which uses TransUnion data to give you a weekly evaluation of your credit score.

It allows you to predict and calculate a cause-and-effect situation if you paid all debts or made payments on time for either 6 or 12 months and so on.

It is available to Capital One bank customers using any of their credit cards.

Chapter 8: Checking Your Credit Report

Checking your credit report regularly is important—it not only can help to prevent errors that may cause you to be denied access to new credit but also can help uncover whether or not you've been a victim of identity theft. And last, but not least, since your credit score is based on the information contained within your credit reports, it's important to make sure that there are no errors on them that could lead to a lowered credit score.

Checking your credit reports can be a chore, but with the right information, you'll see that getting your hands on your reports and checking them over is fast and easy!

Where to Obtain Your Credit Report

Go to www.AnnualCreditReport.com to get your credit report. This is the only website that is authorized by Federal law to provide you with the free credit report that the law entitles you to. While you will find many other websites that offer free credit reports, there are often strings attached.

How Often Are You Allowed a Free Copy of Your Credit Report?

By law, you are allowed to access your credit report for free once per year, from each of the big three credit reporting agencies. You are also entitled to a free copy of your credit report if any of the following occur:

- You are unemployed but plan on looking for a job within 60 days.
- You're on welfare.
- Your report contains errors due to fraud (for example, identity theft).

Hot Tip: Avoid paying for pricey credit monitoring services by staggering your credit report requests instead. Ask for a report from Equifax in January, Experian in May, and TransUnion in September. For most people, this is a great way of monitoring your credit for free.

Remember: Although you are entitled to a free copy of your credit report periodically, you are not entitled to a free copy of your credit score—the credit reporting agencies, including FICO, are allowed to charge you for that.

Your 6-Step Credit Check Checklist

Now that you know where to get your credit report, here are the six steps to successfully checking it over.

Verify that your name, address, date of birth, and social security number are accurate

Be on the lookout for name confusion. For example, Mike Smith or Michael Smith is likely ok, but Michael Smith II and Michael Smith I could be totally different people. Ditto for Jr. and Sr. If either of these scenarios applies to you, be sure your credit report shows the correct title.

Read over the guide to interpreting a credit report that is provided by the credit bureau

Credit reports often have codes that make no sense to a first-time user. Save yourself the frustration of reading their "foreign language" by reading through the user guide or help files that explain how to interpret the information and codes contained in your report.

I'll admit that it's dull and boring to read through the guide, but it'll be well worth it since it will save you tons of time when reading through your report. And besides, if you check your credit report regularly (and you should!), with time, the information contained in the guide will become committed to memory.

Look for any errors in account activity

According to the US Government Accountability Office, 25% of all credit reports have errors, and about half of those errors are affecting the credit score. When you look over your credit reports, ensure that there isn't any incorrect information, such as claims that you paid late when you didn't.

Pay particular attention to any negative account activity, such as late or missed payments—if the information is accurate, so be it. But if the negative information is not correct, you can have it fixed.

Look for accounts that do not belong to you

Make sure all of the accounts listed on your report actually belong to you. Sometimes simple errors in Social Security numbers or misspelled names can lead to someone else's account information showing up on your report.

Check for duplicate accounts

Sometimes if an account is transferred from one company to another, due to a merger, for example, the account ends up on your credit report twice—once under each company name. This can lead to your amount of available credit being reported inaccurately.

Look for lines of credit that are inactive

If you have lines of credit that are no longer needed, it may be worth closing them to "make room" for a new credit application somewhere else. However, I only recommend doing this if you need to since having unused credit can improve your credit score by helping to keep your credit utilization percentage lower.

The 2 Things You Must Do If You Find Errors on Your Credit Report

If you find any errors, here are the two steps that you must take to fix them. The error may be an innocent mistake or a sign of something more serious such as identity theft—either way, you need to find out and fix it.

- In writing, inform the credit reporting agency that is showing an error on their report. Unless they consider your request frivolous, they are generally required to investigate within 30 days. To expedite the process, provide them with all the information (copies, not originals!) they could possibly need from you to begin their investigation.
- In writing, inform the company that provided the inaccurate information to the credit reporting agency that they made an error and you are formally requesting an investigation. Provide them with all relevant information in your

possession that proves the accuracy of your claim. Again, send copies, not originals, of any documentation that you provide.

Expert Tips

Expert Tip #1

Even if a credit reporting agency allows you to report an issue via telephone, this may not be your best option. Ideally, you ought to have copies of all correspondence so that you can refer to them if things get lost. Make photocopies of all written correspondence, save copies of any e-mails that you send, and take screenshots of any information you provide via online Contact Us forms.

To take a screenshot on a PC, press and hold the Alt button while you press the Print Screen key. The Print Screen key is located near the upper-right corner of your keyboard.

To take a screenshot on a Mac, press Command + Shift + 4 at the same time. Then drag the cursor to capture the portion of the screen that you wish to save a picture of.

Expert Tip #2

When mailing documentation, pay extra for the service that provides you with proof of delivery. This way, you'll be 100% certain that the information was received on time.

If you win your claim, the company that reported the inaccurate information must inform all three major credit bureaus of the error. In addition to that, the credit reporting agency whose report showed the error must provide you a corrected copy of your credit report for free.

Once the credit reporting agency agrees to correct the error, it could take a few weeks for the change to show up. If you require the correction to occur sooner in order to facilitate your approval for a loan, ask your lender about a rapid rescore. This service isn't available directly to consumers, but to lenders—it often allows for credit scores to be corrected within days.

So, say you're applying for a mortgage and correcting an error could lead to an increase in your score and a better interest rate for your mortgage. If you can provide your lender with proof of the error, they may be able to expedite a rapid rescore for you (extra fees may apply).

However, there are no guarantees that you'll be granted a rapid rescore, so the best option is to check over your credit reports a few months in advance and allow lots of time for any errors to be investigated and corrected.

5 Bonus Tips

1. If you are checking your credit report to verify accuracy before obtaining credit, be sure to ask the creditor which reports and scores system they use so you can check those first. You might as well start with the most important credit reports.
2. If you're like most people, checking each of your three credit reports once a year will be plenty to keep on top of things. As for your actual credit score, according to FICO, in a three-month period, 75% of people have a change in their credit score of fewer than 20 points—in other words, for most people, the month-to-month changes in their credit scores are relatively small. So, it's probably not worth paying for

access to your credit score too often, unless you need to know your number to double-check what kind of shape, you're in.
3. Generally speaking, collection accounts should be removed from your credit report after seven years—if you see any older than that, contact the relevant credit reporting agency and ask if it can be removed.
4. Don't worry if you see a bunch of "Account Management" or "Account Maintenance" inquiries from your credit card company—it is perfectly normal for them to check your credit reports periodically, and these checks will not affect your credit score.
5. To check up on your FICO score, look at my FICO report—it will even tell you what negative factors might be affecting your score. You can order your score on their website: www.myfico.com

You've now learned how to get your hands on your credit report, how to check it over, and what to do if you find any mistakes.

Action Steps

- Go to www.AnnualCreditReport.com and get your free credit report. Remember, unless there are extenuating circumstances, it's best to stagger your credit report orders so that you can check one every four months. For example, check Equifax in January, Experian in May, and TransUnion in September.
- Go through the 6-step credit check checklist and verify the accuracy of the information on your credit report.
- If you find any errors, take action to correct them.

Chapter 9: The Right Mindset for Credit Management

Realization of Your Current Mindset

Before you start to make any changes, you need to know where your mindset sits at this moment. Think of how you feel when you ponder about your credit card debt as this will tell you more about your mindset than you might realize.

If you are like most people, you feel frustrated about your current situation. How you got into credit card debt will depend on what you are saying to yourself. For example, you might be angry or blame yourself for getting into debt. You might ask yourself why you allowed this situation to happen.

No matter what you notice about your current mindset, you need to accept it and understand why you feel this way. You also need to understand that it is okay for you to feel like this as it will help you reach the get-out-of-debt mindset.

Don't Forget About Gratitude

Debt can cause us to become resentful. We often see other people enjoy the luxuries of life, whether it is by purchasing a new vehicle or going on a vacation. You might even feel resentful because they are able to afford new clothes. One of the best ways to get out of the negative mindset that is attached to credit card debt is to let go of your resentment and focus on gratitude.

Look around your home to see all the wonderful items that you own. Try to think about how lucky you are when it comes to your family, friends, and everyone else who is in your life. You don't always need to focus on the bigger things; sometimes looking at the smaller moments is just as helpful. For example, you may feel gratitude when your child smiles at you while they are playing quietly with their toys.

If you struggle with gratitude, one of the best techniques is writing down what you are grateful for at the end of every day. Find a journal and write everything that made you feel positive. You can also point out what bad things happened but try to find a way you can learn from them or turn them into something a little positive.

Take Responsibility for Your Debt

There is a big difference between blaming yourself for your credit card debt and taking responsibility for it. The biggest difference is what type of mindset you are in. For instance, if you are asking yourself how you could have been so dumb to allow yourself to obtain so many credit cards, you are blaming yourself for what happened. Instead, you need to take responsibility, which means you should try saying something like this to yourself: "I know I got myself into debt because I took out too many credit cards. Now, how can I start to pay off my credit card debt?"

Taking responsibility helps put you in the right mindset because it helps you realize that while you made a mistake, you understand the error, and you are ready to solve the problem. On top of this, you should always look at how you can keep yourself from making the same mistake again. No matter how you get yourself out of credit card debt, they are always going to be tempting.

Stop Seeing Debt-Free as a Solution to Your Problem

Another step you want to take to prepare yourself for your mindset to get out of debt is to stop looking at becoming debt-free as the solution to your problem. The reality is that there is probably more than one reason why you are in debt. While you want to avoid blaming yourself, you also need to take responsibility for your mistakes.

Therefore, write down all the ways that you can become free of debt. This might mean that you should close all your credit cards and work on a plan to pay them off on time, or it may also mean that you should get a second job to help pay off your debt quickly. Instead of thinking about becoming debt-free as the only solution, you need to think of it as the outcome. You need to make becoming debt-free or having financial freedom be your ultimate goal. You should work on coming up with a series of steps that will help you reach your goal.

For example, let's assume that you're a college student who has opened up five credit cards. You are soon graduating and know that you need to start paying off all your smaller debt because you will be paying off student loans in the very near future. Therefore, you decide that one of your best options is to pay off your credit cards and no longer allow yourself to use them. Therefore, you work to think about how you can pay off your five credit cards in a single year.

Next, you think about all the tips you receive from your job as a waitress. Typically, you bring home anywhere from $100 to $300, depending on the night and how busy it is. You realize that you can put all your tip money toward paying off your credit cards. This will allow you to pay off your debt faster. After doing the math, you realize that all your credit cards will be paid off in full by the time your student loans will begin needing to be paid. Through your planning, you started to see becoming debt-free from credit cards as your outcome instead of your solution. By doing this, you were able to come up with a logical solution that works, provided that you are able to follow it over the year.

Your Get-out-of-Debt Mindset

Reframe Your Thoughts

Another major step for your mindset to get out of debt is to turn your negative thoughts into positive ones. This is one of the biggest reasons that you want to become grateful for what you have in life, including your credit card debt. Even though this might be hard to do right now, it is important to realize that this is a life lesson you are learning. In fact, by taking control of your credit card debt, you will be able to take control of your budget and reach financial freedom. Furthermore, the more negative you are, the less likely you will be to follow your goals and your budget.

Write Down a List of Reasons to Get Out of Debt

Getting out of credit card debt is not going to be easy. In fact, you will need to take steps to keep yourself focused as there will be times you feel frustrated or lack confidence in getting out of debt. One of the ways to overcome this is by writing down a list of reasons for wanting to get out of debt. This list can include anything that comes to your mind. For example, you might write that you want to own a home one day. You might also state that you want to be debt-free within two years. Another reason might be your children will be going to college starting in five years, and you want to be able to help them. It doesn't matter what your reasons are; what really matters is that they are your reasons for getting out of debt.

Realize That People Depend on You

If you have a family, you will want to think about all the people who depend on you for your income. It is a lot easier to be able to go out and buy diapers, groceries, and any other household items you need when you don't have to worry about what debt you are getting into. Instead, you can pay through your debit card or with cash without having to worry about the purchase again.

Set up Automatic Payments

Every credit card company will allow you to set up automatic payments through their website. Some will even set up automatic payments while over the phone. Whatever you need to do, take time to set up these payments. This will help you make sure that these bills are getting paid. The trick is that you want to refrain from canceling or postponing your automatic payments as this is typically an option. Again, this is something that you can put into your plan, so you are less likely to cancel.

Find Ways to Keep You Motivated

While you are creating your get-out-of-debt plan, you want to include ways that will help you stay motivated. Perhaps this means checking your progress every other month to see how much your credit card debt has gone down. For example, if you have five credit cards and you are paying $100 on them every month, you will see they have gone down close to $200 every two months. If you add this up, you have decreased your total credit card debt by $1,000. You can decide to track your progress through a spreadsheet on your computer or via a journal. Note the amount you owe when you pay and then notice the new amount the next time you make a payment.

Know That You Can Do It

Sometimes we struggle to follow through with our debt-free plan because we feel like we can't achieve it. It is important to note that there will be times you feel this way. There will be moments when you feel like you can't continue to focus on paying off your debt. You might look and see that you still have two years of credit card debt to pay off and that your other bills continue to pile up.

Establish a Reward System

The fact is you will find yourself struggling to maintain your mindset to get out of debt from time to time. This might not be because you want to purchase something that you can't afford, but rather it may be because you find yourself getting tired of seeing how much money you owe because of credit cards.

Conclusion

If you want to repair your credit, then here are some steps that might be more effective. The first step is to gather your finances together and make a budget. Sometimes the problem isn't about paying what you owe so much as it is about priorities. Next, save up an emergency fund of at least $1000 in case of any unexpected expenses that pop up in the future. Next, tackle the collection agencies. Many of them will work with you if you explain your situation, and are willing to pay less than the full amount if you can afford it. It might be worth looking into a credit counselor as sometimes they can help with creditors and make things easier on your financial situation.

Credit repair service is a process that creates an accurate financial history for a customer and helps to increase their credit score. One of the ways in which your credit score can be increased is by obtaining new loans, paying off old loans, and making payments on time. A good credit score will give you access to better interest rates as well as other financial services.

Your credit score will be scarred regardless if they fix it or not. And, because the credit repair company is charging you a fee to fix your score, the chances are that you will have to pay for their services in the future. There are many websites out there that will list top credit repair companies, and while some of them do work, some of them are just trying to get your money. In addition, some people think the credit repair companies are legitimate and then end up paying for their services anyways. It is the easiest solution because you can pick up phone calls from these companies, but be careful. You have to make sure that you do not give any personal contact information to these credit repair companies because they are fakes. If you want to use a credit repair company, do some research on your own before you give them any personal information. Also, check the state department's website for complaints against the company. If there are hundreds of complaints that they are a scamming company, then do not give them any money. Trust me, it is better to be safe than sorry.

You may be in denial about the state of your credit, but if you are planning on applying for any loans or credit cards, you must try and fix them. Nowadays people rely on their credit scores more than ever before to determine their eligibility for loans and other types of credit. Such companies are highly skilled in the art of repairing credit and can help you avoid some of the most common pitfalls. If you have suffered a serious hit to your score due to late payments or bankruptcies, it could take years before your score is restored to its former glory. That's because it takes time for your creditors to update their records with your current status, you should pay off any outstanding debts and make your payments on time. If you have made a few late payments recently, or have otherwise damaged your credit score, contact the creditor or consumer reporting agency. Explain that you have had some trouble recently, but you are now working to rectify the situation and would like to make a payment arrangement. Many creditors and agencies will work with consumers who show a sincere desire to repay their debts.

Finally, my opinion on the best way to improve your credit is to make a budget for yourself and stick to it! If you can avoid doing that, then your credit will be in great shape.

BOOK 2
HOW TO BOOST YOUR CREDIT SCORE

Take Revenge On Those Who Didn't Think You Could Afford That Expensive Car or Home. Fix Your Bad Credit Score in Less Than 30 Days and Live The Life You Deserve!

Introduction

Your credit score is a simple three-digit number used to judge your creditworthiness as a customer. It is calculated by using your credit history. From lenders to prospective employers and other financial institutions, various third parties use your credit score. It is used to determine whether you can repay your debts or not. The credit score can range from 300 to 850. The higher the credit score, the greater is one's financial stability. Fair Isaac Corporation is accredited with the creation of the credit score model. It is also known as FICO and is used by various financial institutions. There are a couple of other credit scoring models too. Still, FICO is the most popular and commonly used model these days.

You can maintain a high credit score by ensuring you have a history of timely payment of bills and by maintaining a low debt level. There are various factors, which influence your credit score. A credit score is one of the critical criteria evaluated by a lender while offering credit to prospective borrowers. A credit score of less than 640 is considered to be subprime. From a lender's perspective, the lower is your credit score; the higher is the risk of default. So, the rates charged by financial institutions on loans increase as the credit score decreases. According to FICO, a credit score between 800 and 850 is believed to be excellent while the one between 300 and 579 is reduced. The good news is regardless of what your credit score is, you can work on improving it.

Benefits of a Good Credit Score

The dependency on credit for making purchases is growing by the day in modern society. Good credit is no longer just used for securing a loan or even getting a credit card. The list of businesses using your credit score to determine their decision about extending their products or services to you is steadily increasing.

Interest rates

The interest you pay is the cost of acquiring credit or borrowing any money. Apart from repaying the principal amount you borrowed, you must also pay attention to the creditor or the lender. Your credit score influences the interest rate chargeable. A good credit score means you can qualify for the best interest rate in the market. So, it directly helps reduce the finance charges on loans or credit balances.

- **Qualify for credit**

Borrowers with a history of poor credit usually avoid applying for new sources of loans or praise because they were turned down in the past. If you have a good credit score, it does not necessarily guarantee you will be approved for a loan, because other factors will be considered like your level of debt as well as income. However, an excellent credit score certainly increases the chances of approval. So, if you are looking to secure a new source of credit, then you can apply for it confidently if you have a good credit score.

- **Power to negotiate**

When you have a good credit score, it gives you the power to negotiate a lower interest rate while securing new lines of credit. By leveraging your ability to negotiate, you can make the most of all the competitive offers you get from other companies according to your credit score. On the other hand, with a low credit score, the lenders will be stricter and more rigid with the terms of loans. Also, the number of options available to you will decrease.

- **Borrow more**

Your credit score and earning capacity determine your borrowing capacity. When you have a good credit score, lenders will be more comfortable allowing you to borrow more because of your history of prompt repayment. Even with a poor credit score, you will be able to borrow, but you might not qualify for higher limits.

- **Properties**

These days, landlords have started to use credit scores while screening potential tenants. A poor credit score caused due to any prior evictions or outstanding rents can harm your chances of renting a property. A good credit score gives the landlords confidence about your ability to pay the rent on time and not default on rental payments. So, if you want less hassle while searching for a rental property, you must work on improving your credit score.

- **Car insurance**

Various companies that provide auto insurance use credit scores to determine the premium payable by policyholders. In the insurance circle, it is a widespread belief that an individual with a poor credit score is going to file for more insurance claims. Therefore, they charge a higher premium for such people. Cell phone

A bad credit score can directly influence your ability to get a cell phone on a contractual basis. Cell phone service providers are often wary of all those who have a bad credit score. If pay-as-you-go plans hold little appeal to you, then work on fixing your credit score. Also, if you have a good credit score, you might be allowed a little slack. You might not have to pay any security deposit while getting a cellphone on a contractual basis.

- **Utilities**

The deposits payable on utility services can be anywhere between $100 and $200. It can be a costly expenditure while you are relocating. You might not have any plans of relocating right now, but if you do have to in the future, then a good credit score will come in handy. A good credit score means you do not have to pay any security deposit while transferring a utility service to a new location or while obtaining a new utility service.

You can certainly survive with poor credit, but it will prove to be rather expensive and complicated. By maintaining a good credit score, you can reduce your financial stress.

Chapter 1: Pay Your Debts

Remember that you need to focus on paying off all your debts at the earliest. You cannot waste any more time and must try and finish them off to have a good score. Let us now look at the things that you need to do to pay off your debts on time.

You can pay off your debts in one of the two methods that are made available viz. the first one being the avalanche method and the second being the snowball method. Each type has its own advantages and disadvantages. You need to look at whatever fits your budget best and go for it without wasting any more time. If you think you have enough money saved up, then choose the avalanche method but if you have very little then chosen the snowballing method. Apart from these, if you have enough money to pay for everything altogether then you can choose that option as well.

Planning

Remember to always work with a plan. When you have everything planned out it will be easy for you to finish your task. Start by preparing a monthly budget by including your incomes and expenses and try and balance it out to remain with as much money at the end as possible. You need to add your debts to the expenses column and this will help you pay them on time. When you are left with a surplus, you can use it to open a separate "debt repayment" account and add in the money there. Once you have a substantial amount, you can use it to pay off all your debts.

Organizing

Mere planning will not suffice and you need to be as organized as possible. You must have everything in place to help you operate smoothly. Try having a different account for each of your debts so that money automatically gets transferred every month. You must also have a set monthly budget for your expenses. You must not use any more money than what you have assigned. When you are organized, you will feel that your life is easy and there are not many obstacles standing in your way.

Contact

Many times, it pays to develop a good rapport with your creditors. But don't push it and remain within your limits. You need to develop a rapport and not a close friendship with them. You need to win over their trust and make them like your determination. Remain in touch with them and update them on your every move to repay their debts on time. After a while, the informality between the two of you will start to reduce.

Negotiate

When you have struck a good rapport, you can decide to ask for a small rebate in your debt or negotiate the rate of interest that you have to pay. This might not be possible with all creditors such as banks but you can try your luck with moneylenders and other non-commercial lenders. Once they are happy with your timely debt repayments, they might decide to reduce the interest rate by a little. But don't expect them to waive off your loan as nobody will be willing to do that. You can ask them if you can pay a little less for the last few installments and count that as your rebate.

Secured Credit Card

When you are trying to pay off all your debts at the earliest, you must not use your credit card excessively. Your credit score will plummet and so, you should give up on these. There are alternatives to credit cards that you can consider. Debit cards are a great idea as you will only draw money from your own account when you use these. But if you want to have the feel of a credit card then you can opt for a secured credit card. These are issued by your bank and they will be linked to your account. You will have to add money to this account and there will be a limit on how much you can draw in a month. There will be no interest levied on the amount and you must add back the money that you withdrew within a specified time to help the account remain active.

Family

Sometimes, if there is a lot of debt then you can consider borrowing some money from your relatives. When you do so, you will be able to pay off a debt easily. Your family members might not charge you a high rate of interest and it might be within your budget. You can consider asking your dad or your uncle or anybody who is in a position to pay you the amount at the earliest. You need not stress over paying the sum back to them and can do it leisurely and at your own pace.

Life Insurance

It is also possible for you to borrow money from your life insurance policy. You can ask for a certain amount that you promise to pay back within a specified time. There is no interest as such that will be levied on this sum and you can repay it after a few years' time.

Once you repay your debt and give back to your insurance company then you will truly be free and your credit score will start to rise high.

Bank Borrowing

It pays to have everything unified to make easy payments. This means that you can borrow a certain amount from your bank and pay off all your creditors in bulk. You can then pay only to your bank to settle your debts. This will make it easier for you as you have to pay to only one institution. The rate of interest might also be low and that will help you save on a lot of money. The only disadvantage of this type is that not many banks entertain this sort of borrowing. However, you can try your luck and approach two or more banks with a proposal.

Money Savers

Every month, think of ways in which you can save on money. This can be by way of using coupons while shopping or making use of store credit to help save on the bill etc. You can also sell your old and unused stuff to make some money out of it. Nevertheless, if you cannot gift a service every time then you can consider buying them in bulk after the holiday is over and store them to be gifted the next year. Cutting down on electricity, water, and gas bills will also help you save money. It is also ideal for you to buy second-hand goods for the time being and save further.

You can follow these steps to repay all your loans at the earliest and improve your credit score.

Chapter 2: Delete Bad Credit Legally

Public records that appear on your credit report include civil judgments, tax liens, and bankruptcy filings.

Tax Liens

The federal government has a Fresh Start program that makes this process fairly straightforward. To qualify you are going to need to be current on your taxes and have received a Release of Tax Lien document. You will also need the original form that provided notice of the lien in the first place. You will then need to fill out IRS form 12277 Application for Withdrawal of Filed Form 688Y, available at IRS.gov. You will then need to submit this, along with your original form and proof that you have paid off the lien to the IRS.

Judgments

Having a judgment on your credit report can be nearly as harmful as having a repossession or a loan default. While removing a judgment is possible, it is not as easy as removing a late payment or a credit inquiry. A judgment shows up on your credit report if a judge signs off on a statement saying that you owe a specific debt. This occurs when a lawsuit is filed against you to collect a debt, even if you weren't aware of the court proceedings at the time. It is important to keep in mind that just because a judgment was issued against you, that doesn't mean the other party was paid, which is a fact that you will use to your advantage.

There are two different ways to deal with a judgment once it has hit your credit report, you can have the judgment dismissed, also known as vacated, or remove the judgment from your credit report.

Dismiss A Judgment

In order to have a judgment dismissed, you need to file a motion to dismiss the judgment with the court that issued the judgment in the first place. This is essentially an appeal that states the original outcome was inaccurate or unfair based on a specific number of reasons. First, you will want to look through the proceedings and ensure that the person who requested the judgment in the first place went ahead and followed all the correct procedures and laws for doing so in your area. If there was mismanagement of this process, the odds are that the judge didn't know about it when the judgment was made.

In addition to following up on the judgment process, you will need to ensure that the person filing the judgment also followed proper court proceedings as you may be able to win out based on a technicality. This is especially important if you failed to show up for your court date and the plaintiff won by default as long as you had a valid reason for not showing up for the hearing in the first place. Again, it is important to familiarize yourself with local laws for this process to be effective.

When you prepare your motion to vacate you must follow local rules for the civil procedure to the letter, the rules for your area should spell out exactly what you need to do, explain valid reasons a judgment can be vacated, and will often include specific language you will need to use to file your motion.

The document you create should explain why the judgment should be vacated, starting with the reasons why you are bringing the motion forward. You will need to state your procedural defense and explain why you missed the original hearing if that is what happened. Valid reasons include that you were not served properly, that you responded to the summons but there was no initial judgment or that you did not have time to make it to the hearing based on when you were served. There may be other valid reasons in your area as well.

You will also need to include reasons why the judgment would have been dismissed if you had been at the hearing including things like, the collection agency failed to respond to your validation request or that the debt amount exceed local usury interest limits.

Bankruptcy

Removing a bankruptcy from your credit report is the most difficult black mark to remove. While it is far from a sure thing, a general rule is that the older the bankruptcy is, the easier it is to remove. To get started you are going to want to look for errors relating to it, if there are then you are in luck. If you find errors, you can go about asking the bureau to remove them in the standard way.

Regardless of the information is accurate or not, you are still going to want to ask the bureau to verify the bankruptcy as they will be unlikely to go about doing it in the right way. Assuming they come back and tell you that it has been verified by one court or another, this is almost always inaccurate as courts rarely verify bankruptcies. With this information in hand, you will want to reach out to the court that has been specified and ask them how they verify bankruptcies. You can call and ask for this information, typically from the clerk of the court. Assuming they explain that they don't verify bankruptcies you will then want to get that fact in writing.

When you receive this letter in the mail, you will then want to send it to the bureau that claimed to have verified your bankruptcy in the first place along with a letter explaining what it is and stating that, as the bankruptcy was not actually verified, you want it taken off your record as by not doing so earlier, but saying that they did, they are in direct violation of the FCRA.

Deletion of Negative Public Records (Judgments)

Ever had your wages garnished?

I did—I fought—I won

I had to pay a settlement, but I got the judgment VACATED from the clerk of court and removed completely from my credit record.

Garnishments are the worst thing for your credit, you don't want this on your report, and any potential employers will have a serious problem with this.

I used whatever leverage I could find and wrote a letter to the Judge that handled the case and explained in lengthy detail how it all happened, why the creditor was being too harsh and ruthless, and what violations I believed he committed.

The Judge actually ruled in my favor for the second hearing which I could not attend due to work, I gave my letter to the bailiff before the court date.

I still had to pay court costs but I won. I wasn't even there, and the Creditor's attorney was very upset, apparently, losing the case really made him look bad to the firms' Partners.

Public Records will require serious measures to get vacated or deleted. Keep in mind anything is negotiable if you can find the leverage or violation within the Fair Credit Acts. Most of the time they are there, but you have to look very hard.

In addition, getting creditors to vacate or delete a public judgment can be accomplished with settlements and negotiations while leveraging the Fair Credit Acts. Where there is a will there is a way. Do you think attorneys give up when the odds are stacked against their case? No way, they find loopholes and any leverage they can find—I would suggest you view defending your credit report the same way, only the consumer laws are MORE biased for you.

Chapter 3: Write A Credit Repair Letter 609

Whether you want to delete just one thing from your record or you are looking to delete a lot of different things at the same time, you want to make sure that your 609 Letter is taken care of and ready to go. There are a lot of parts that need to go through to get this done, but when you look at some of the templates, you will see that this is not as bad as it may seem.

When you are ready to write out some of the letters you need to send out to the credit agencies, and you are getting all of the documentation ready to go, make sure to follow some of the general advice that we have below:

Keep All of the Records

Everything has to be recorded on your end of things. Don't just send out a letter and then assume that it is going to be all good. You never know when things are going to go missing or when you will need to prove your side of things. And the more accurate and in-depth records you can take, the better it will be with everyone. This means that we need to keep track of everything, from the moment that we start sending out information and letters to the credit bureaus all the way until way after the fact when they take that information off your credit report. This will help you if anything comes back later on, or you need to make sure that you can prove your side of the story if the credit agency doesn't respond or do what they are supposed to.

Keep track of everything that you can along the way. You should have all of the letters that you send out, both the originals and any follow-ups that you send as well. If the credit agency gets back in touch with you, then you should keep the letters they send to you and your responses back. You can hold onto all of the supporting documents that you send each time as well. The more information that you add to your records about this, the better it will be for getting your way in the process.

Add in the Identification Information

Before you send out any information or work with section 609, make sure that you send along with it some identification information. This is going to make sure that the credit agency is going to understand who you are and can prove that they are actually working with the person who says they own the account or at least own the SSN that goes with all that information on the credit report.

There are a lot of different options that you are able to use for showing your identity, and you should include a number of them with your letter to help prove who you are. You would want to work with information like your driver's license, social security numbers, and more to showcase who you are and why you need to make a difference in the credit report.

Consider Bringing Something Up, even if it Doesn't Seem Important

While you are at this process, it is worth bringing up even some of the smaller things that are on your report. Even if these don't seem important at the time, and they are not the main thing that you want to put your time and attention are, while you are writing the letter, you should add in as many details and as many disputes that are legitimate as possible.

You never know what you would be able to get erased off the credit report, and how much of a difference that is going to make to your credit score along the way. Even if the item seems small, you should consider adding it to the dispute that you will do.

Sometimes, the time limit will go on too long, and the agency will not respond. If this happens, all of the items, whether they are big or small, will need to be taken out of the report. And you will find that even a few small things can add up to be big things in the long run. Even if the credit agency won't erase all of the little things, it doesn't really take much of a difference along the way in terms of the time that you take to get it all done. And it could make a difference.

Do Not Contact the FTC

One thing that a lot of people are going to try and use is to contact the FTC and other agencies in the hope of getting things fixed. They may hope that because there is something wrong with the credit report, the FTC will be able to help them take care of this. Sometimes they are mad and want to get the agency in trouble for falsely adding things to their reports. And other times, they may just not know who they are supposed to contact.

However, this is not going to do you any good. If you contact the FTC, they are not going to be able to provide you with the assistance that you need. In fact, their stance is that they are not going to get in between you and the credit agency at all, and all you will get back is a form letter stating these facts. Since you have other options at your disposal to work with, you do not need to work with the FTC, but just make sure that you are going to not waste time in the process.

When you want to get something on your credit report fixed and all better, then it is important to not waste time with the FTC, and instead go straight to the credit agencies. You can send the same letter and the same information to each one, and they are the ones who will be able to help us to get things done. If you follow the rules that we are using here, and some of the other steps that we talked about, you will be able to get your credit report taken care of.

Send a Letter to Each Credit Agency

One thing that we need to remember here is that we have to go through the process of sending out one of these Section 609 letters to each credit agency that we want to get to remove the items. The credit agencies are not going to talk to one another about this. If you send out a letter to Transunion, but not to one of the others, then Transunion may take it off your report, but none of the others would do this for you.

You have to be responsible for sending a letter to all three of the reporting agencies if you would like to get that debt taken out of all of your reports. You should automatically send this information to all three right from the start, so make sure to get copies of all the information so that you are ready to go and handle all of that at once as well.

You can include the same information in each of the letters that you send out. And you can even send out the same letter, just make sure to change the company and department name that you are using on each one. Then include the same proofs of your identity, the credit reports, and more, for each one to get the ball rolling here.

Mention Section 609 in the Letter

There are a few different things that we need to remember when it comes to writing out our form letters. We need to include our name and some of the information about who we are and where we live. We need to include information about the debts and accounts that we would like to dispute along the way, including a credit report to show what accounts were talking about. And then we need to make sure that we, at some point, mention section 609 in the letter. This is going to be useful in several aspects. First, it is going to show the credit agency that you know what you are talking about. There are a lot of people out there who would like to fix their credit scores, but they don't understand the laws, or they are trying to sneak things past. The credit agencies are going to notice these individuals easily and will not want to work with them at all. But when you go through and mention Section 609 in your letter, like we have talked about so far in this book, then you will find that it is much easier for you to grab their attention. You actually have done your research, you know what your rights are, and you are ready to take them on to get the credit report taken care of. The credit agencies are going to notice and respect this, and that will make it more likely that they will listen to you and send out the information that you need or erase the information that should not be there.

Mention the 30-Day Limit

In addition to making sure that you mention something about Section 609 in the letter you send out, you need to also make sure that you mention the 30 days that the agency gets to respond to you. This not only helps to show that you have a good idea about what you are talking about here but will make it easier for you to remind the credit agency about this right that you have with Section 609 that we talk about here. The letters that we have below will have examples of how you are able to write these out in your own form letter. But make sure to mention this and that you expect the credit agency to respond and work with that time limit in order to get things taken care of. If you do this, then it is a lot harder for them to come back with not knowing about the time limit and sets out the same expectations that everyone on both sides needs to follow.

Use One of the Templates So You Know Where to Start

Making sure that you have included all of the right parts in your letter is going to be a challenge. You want to make sure that you write it out in the right manner, that you mention the right parts about Section 609, and you want to make sure that you sound like you know what you are talking about along the way. The good news is that we have provided some templates that we are able to use in order to take care of this process.

Send a Follow-Up Letter

We may think that all of the work is done, and we won't have to do anything else after we send off the initial letter to all three credit agencies. But unfortunately, there are a few other steps that we need to complete. Once you are certain that the 30 days have passed and you have given the company enough time to respond to what you sent in, it is time to send in the follow-up a letter telling them that it is now their responsibility to remove that information from your credit report.

This basically will tell the agency that you sent in information about the different disputes you had on your credit report, and since they have not replied in the timely manner given by the FRCA in Section 609, it is now time for them to remove those items from your credit report.

These letters are short and sweet and will not have a lot to them. They will summarize some of the information that you sent out to them a month ago, and then reiterate what your rights are under Section 609 and what you expect the credit agency to do now that the right amount of time has passed. Depending on the length of your original dispute, this letter could be long or short.

There are a lot of misconceptions out there when it comes to working with the Section 609 letter, and getting it right is going to make the difference between whether you are able to get the credit agency to do what you would like, which would then increase your credit score, or not. Following the advice here will help to make this whole process easier as well.

Chapter 4: Delete Inquiries Like a Pro

An inquiry is when a creditor, employer, or insurance company request to view and examine your credit reports via TransUnion, Equifax, or Experian. You have soft inquiries and hard inquiries, a hard inquiry is when you give consent to any potential creditor to pull your credit reports, and too many hard inquiries will hurt your score. Soft Inquiries are also referred to as a soft pull, this is when you check your own credit, or credit card companies want to look at your score to solicit you for pre-approval offers.

Current creditors often perform soft pulls to issue periodic credit line increases. These acts are both documented by the credit bureaus, no need for you to worry about soft pulls; they will not hurt your credit score no matter how many times you check your own credit. You can opt-out to prevent others from looking at your reports through soft pulls. Hard inquiries will be kept on your credit report for a period of up to 25 months. Allowing too many creditors to pull your credit within a short time will damage your chances for new credit as each inquiry can cost you 3–5 points of your fico score, it is best to have no more than 5 inquiries reporting at a time on each credit bureau. Applying for too many accounts will result in you looking too thirsty to obtain credit. The longer an inquiry sits on your credit report, the less it impacts your fico score, but too many recent inquiries will get you automatic denials in the computer underwriting systems of most banks and credit card issuers.

It is never a good idea to request any form of credit before you plan on financing any big purchase, especially a mortgage. Every point count when you are looking for low-interest rates on long-term loans. Another way to control inquiries is to understand which credit report will be pulled by certain creditors; you can even direct certain creditors to pull from a bureau of your favor by freezing the others and applying by phone. Perhaps you have the highest score with Equifax, and you know a specific lender that pulls both Equifax and Experian, it would be wise for you to freeze Experian that has the lower fico score, and this allows easy access to your Equifax. Applying for enough credit over the years, I created my own database of which credit bureaus lenders pull from, which can also depend on your city and state. You can also legally freeze and unfreeze any of your credit reports at any time online or over the phone.

It is very common to see files of clients that have 10, 15, or even 20 inquiries on each credit bureau. Either they have let a car dealership or multiple car dealerships run their credit through multiple banks, or they crossed their fingers and applied for any and every credit line they could think of. Either way, with computers processing most applications, this can be an automatic denial for many credit products, especially for credit cards and loans from prime issuers. Too many recent inquiries only show lenders you are desperate for credit, and banks only lend money to those who appear to not really need it. For those who do have any inquiries, you don't necessarily have to wait 2 years for them to fall off; you can actually question their legitimacy and request that the credit bureaus delete them.

With this being said, it is tough for any credit bureau to prove that you actually permitted for a creditor to view your credit report, especially without a physical application. Once they forward the dispute to the furnisher, that creditor really doesn't have any interest in going back and forth with you over this disputed inquiry. Once again, they have bigger fish to fry; they have to worry more about those who actually do owe them some money. Most consumers apply online or on the phone these days for accounts, so these furnishers can't provide any physical proof that you actually did initiate the inquiry. If you write and send your dispute by mail for multiple inquiries, make sure it is with a demand letter to the credit bureaus first; it can become costly sending certified mail to multiple creditors individually. You can formulate your letter and ask for these 3 simple things:

- Permissible purpose.
- Proof that the consumer initiated the inquiry.
- Written authorization.

Those who pulled your credit cannot provide these three things unless you have an account attached to the inquiry, and if so, I advise that you count your blessings for the approval and don't try to remove it.

Remember, anytime you are disputing inquires you are standing because an application in your name was unauthorized, if for any reason you are being ignored or they refuse to delete, you can send a 605B Identity Theft related letter with the support of an automated police report listing all inquiries you are disputing. If you call to dispute, depending on who helps you over the phone, they will want you to report the inquiries as fraudulent, then forward you to the fraud department anyway. After disputing the inquiries, you will have what is called a fraud alert on your credit file as a result. A fraud alert just means that before any credit can be extending to you in the future, they will first have to go through all the necessary steps to assure that you are who you say you are, and not someone attempting to use your identity. If a fraud alert is placed, just remember you will be better off applying for additional credit in person or over the phone until it comes off or you request to delete it by phone that will take up to 48 hours to process. Fraud alerts last 90 days and extended fraud alerts stay on your credit reports for 7 years. Adding your permanent phone number to your fraud alert is the most convenient way to go, I personally suggest that you remove the fraud alert right after you get the inquiries deleted if you plan to submit any applications after. Fraud alerts can help protect your credit otherwise.

With any resistance from the credit bureaus, you can also dispute your inquiries one by one directly with the creditors. They usually won't put up a fight, I prefer to dispute with the credit bureaus first as it is less time demanding than reaching out to every single furnisher responsible for reporting an inquiry if there are many. If for some reason you missed a step or just can't get the results you need, you can threaten or actually sue the furnisher of the inquiry for the violation of section 604 of the FCRA, this violation can reward you with a fine from the defendant. You will never get all the way to court for a matter like this, but as always, have your paper trail.

*Do not repeatedly apply for credit and dispute your inquiries just because you know-how, you want to do everything in moderation to not abuse this tactic for yourself.

"Making more money is not always the answer; some people make 7 figures but still live paycheck to paycheck."

Chapter 5: Recognize and Avoid Common Errors in Your Credit Report

According to the federal trade commission, 1 in 5 Americans has a mistake on their credit report. In other words, approximately 40 million Americans have an error on their credit report; this number is not only astounding but is very revealing. Therefore, a lot of people are being denied credit based on inaccurate information found on their credit files. Also, some people are paying high-interest rates based on errors that were found in their credit reports.

Three common mistakes that cause errors on credit reports:

- Sometimes people inadvertently provide the wrong social security number when applying for credit.
- People sometimes make a mistake when they enter your information on a credit application.
- An account that belongs to John Smith Sr. sometimes will get reported as owned by John Smith Jr.

Note that there could be various mistakes in each of the three credit reports. It is not uncommon to have positive coverage of an account on one article, but poor reports on another.

Most Common Credit Report Errors

Here are others of the most common credit report errors:

- Listed wrong names, emails, or phone numbers.
- Data that refers to another of the same name.
- Duplicate details, whether positive or negative, about the same account.
- Records have negative, apparently positive information.
- Balances on accounts payable are still on view.
- Delinquent payment reports that were never billed in due time.
- This indicates wrong credit limits.
- Claims included in the insolvency which is still due.
- Incorrect activity dates.
- Past-due payments are not payable.
- Court records that are falsely connected with you, such as convictions and bankruptcy.
- Tax liens, not yours.
- Unprecedented foreclosures.
- Incorrect names.
- Wrong address.
- Wrong social security number.
- Accounts not belonging to you.
- Accounts with an incorrect credit limit.
- Open accounts being reported as closed.
- Closed accounts being reported as open.
- Account incorrectly reported as being late.
- Out-dated information.
- The mixture of the two different credit reports.
- Identity theft.
- An account listed twice.

- Incorrect phone number.
- Authorized user listed as the owner of an account.
- Ex-spouse information listed on the credit report.
- Incorrect account status.

How to Prevent Common Errors on Your Credit Report?

It can be very disheartening to discover that you might have errors on your credit report, but taking steps to prevent errors from being placed on your credit report can help you to avoid a lot of unnecessary stress. Take extra caution to secure yourself against identity theft. You should consider setting up credit monitoring alerts to inform you whenever a recent update has been made to your credit report, act fast to correct any errors on your credit report, and double-check any information you provide to a creditor when you apply for credit. Many times, if you have had a long-term account with a creditor, you can contact them directly and explain the error being reported on your credit report.

Ask them to write you a letter with the email and correction. Also, ask them to contact every credit reporting agency that reports this incorrect entry to correct.

Once the creditor receives a copy of the letter, make a copy of it, and attach the letter to the letter of the dispute you send. Mail it to the agency for credit reporting and ask them to update their files. Once that is completed, you will be sent back a new credit report by the credit reporting agency.

Chapter 6: Consider Credit Piggybacking

If you're new to credit or want to make credit mistakes, there are credit cards for people with less than perfect credit. But they are not a good choice for all borrowers because they can have higher interest rates, lower credit limits, and fewer perks than cards for those with strong loans.

One way to work to improve your credit rating without applying for a separate account is to hop on a family member or friend's credit. However, there are things that you should consider before deciding.

What is Credit Piggybacking?

Piggyback uses somebody else's credit card account to improve your credit rating. This usually means that you are added as an authorized user to the credit card of a family member or friend.

According to a 2017 report by the Consumer Financial Protection Bureau, around 11 percent of consumers begin to build up credit with an authorized user account. As an authorized user, you are added to the card account and even receive your own credit card, but you do not need to use it.

Many credit card companies report authorized user accounts to the three national credit bureaus Experian, Equifax, and TransUnion.

Why Piggybacking Can Be Worth It

If you become an authorized user on another person's credit card account, you can build up a balance without the same responsibility you would have if you were to open your own credit card account. Here are some of the benefits:

- You are not liable for the debts. Since you are not the primary or joint account holder, you are not responsible for paying off the credit card each month, even if you were the one who made the purchase. In addition, the credit card company cannot come after you if the primary account holder does not make his payments. Of course, you must repay your family member or friend if you use the card for purchases. Otherwise, it could destroy your relationship.
- The credit card will be displayed on your credit report. When the credit card issuer reports authorized user accounts to the credit bureaus, you will receive the entire positive history on the account. So, if your parents had the same card in the last ten years and you are added as an authorized user, you will immediately have a 10-year account history in your credit report.
- Your exposure to negative history is limited. Your credit score may decrease if the primary cardholder sets up a large balance. However, if that person no longer pays for a while, you can request that the issuer remove you from the account. However, you may also need to verify with the credit bureaus that they have removed the account from your report.

Possible Disadvantages of Credit Piggybacking

The status of an authorized user can help you in the right situation, but there is no guarantee that it will give you the results you want. Here are some of the disadvantages to consider:

Piggybacking is not as useful as having your own account. When FICO published the FICO 8 scoring model in 2009, it announced that authorized user accounts would have less impact on customers' creditworthiness than before. This shift was primarily an attempt to prevent people from using paid piggyback services.

That is, lenders are not required to use the latest scoring models, and some may use even earlier versions. But if you can, you can be more secure with your own credit card or a loan to increase your credit score.

They are delivered to the account holder. If the primary cardholder does not use the card responsibly after adding you as an authorized user—for example, by reaching a high credit or defaulting—this may be poorly reflected in your credit report.

When things get really bad, remember that you can sign out of the account. However, removing the authorized user account from your credit history removes both the positive and negative information associated with the account. So, if you did not take the opportunity to build up your balance in another way, you'll end up starting over.

Other negative elements in your credit report will not be corrected. Adding positive information to your credit reports can help your credit score, but it will not get rid of the negative elements.

"If you have serious delinquency or collection accounts," says Griffin, "these issues will not be offset by an authorized user." So, if you want to restore bad credit, take a look at your credit reports to see what causes it. Focus on first addressing the negative points, including getting involved in payments or paying off high credit card funds. Once you've done these things, an authorized user account can help make a bigger difference.

Beware of paid piggybacking services

Businesses are recruiting people with good credit and paying them to help other people reduce their credit, said Jeff Richardson, vice president and group leader for marketing and communications at VantageScore.

For example, a business calculates up to $ 1,500 depending on the age and credit limit of the account. Once the eligible user account is reported to the credit bureaus, it remains open for two or more months; then, it is "closed" so that the positive account information remains in the credit reports.

According to Richardson, the practice of piggybacking a stranger's credit is frowned upon. "You should not be able to buy good credit," he adds.

What you should know before asking for the status of an authorized user

If done correctly, adding it as an authorized user can help you get the credit score you need to build credit in a different way. But this is a big step for you and your family members or friend. Therefore, it is important that you consider some things before making a decision.

Learn how the credit card issuer reports activity. Not all credit card providers report authorized user accounts and some do not report them at all. Ask your family member or friend to contact the card issuer in advance to find out how the information is communicated to the credit bureaus. If the issuer does not report the information to all three credit bureaus or does not report everything, it is not worth the effort.

Communicate about the arrangement. Although you do not need to use your authorized user card to get the credit benefits of the account, you still want to use it.

"Be very clear and transparent with the person who allows you to be an authorized user," says Richardson. "You take a risk, so clear communication and clear use of the card is essential." Also, make sure you set up an arrangement to repay what you owe when using the card.

Think about all your options. Adding as an authorized user is not always an option. And even if so, it might be more helpful to get your own report. Take the time to consider other options to build up your balance. Richardson recommends that credit for lenders and business and gas credit cards be reviewed. Other options include:

- Apply for a student or a secured credit card.
- Apply for a savings secured loan
- Get a co-signer on a personal or self-loan.
- Ask your landlord to report the rental payments to the credit bureaus.

Perform your due diligence to determine what works best for you.

Also, remember that someone else's piggybacking can only get you this far. Over time, these actions will help you to establish and maintain an excellent credit history for years to come.

Chapter 7: Order A Free Credit Report

Every single American citizen is entitled to one free copy of each of their credit reports every twelve months. The Fair Credit Reporting Act (FCRA) means that TransUnion, Experian, and Equifax are obligated to provide you with these details, but only if you ask for them—you can also obtain a credit report from Innovis. The FCRA promotes the privacy and accuracy of the information from these credit reporting agencies and is enforced by the Federal Trade Commission.

Assuming you visit the website, you will be sent to a form page where you will be required to include pertinent, identifying information including your date of birth, social security number, address, and name. If you have moved within the prior two years, you will probably need to provide your former address as well. Once you submit these details, you will then be taken to a page that will allow you to select the reports you wish to receive, you can choose to get all three at once or to get them one at a time; it doesn't matter, as long as you haven't received them in the preceding 12 months.

You will then be taken to a page that will further help in verifying your identity. You will receive a list of questions about the terms of your loans, your current creditors. You will need to answer all the questions correctly, which means you may need to have your current bill and loan statements handy.

There are pros and cons to pulling all three reports at once, or waiting and spacing them out. If you decide to get your reports one at a time, then you can space them out throughout the year, one every four months, so that you will always be aware when something new affects your credit, negatively or positively. The downside is that if there is something negative on one of your credit reports and not the others, then you will have to wait a full year to find out about it.

On the other hand, pulling all three of your credit reports at the same time will allow you to pinpoint any issues right away, which means you can start working toward a solution for them as soon as possible. Additionally, this method will allow you to determine what the differences between the various reports are and if there are any discrepancies that can be easily resolved such as one of them not showing that you have finished paying off a loan. The downside is, of course, that if something happens to your credit in the next eleven months you won't know about it until the time comes to pull all three reports again. To mitigate this fact, you can sign up with a credit monitoring service, which will monitor your credit for you in between the periods where you are eligible for a free copy of your various reports.

There are many ways to get your free credit report, but the one sponsored by the government is the best and most accurate way to go. You can do this entirely online:

Start by visiting the website www.AnnualCreditReport.com. Then go to:

- Equifax http://www.equifax.com/about-equifax/company-profile
- Experian http://www.experian.com/corporate/about-experian.html

- TransUnion https://www.transunion.com/about-us/about-transunion

You'll have to enter personal information and answer several security questions to verify your identity. Since you are looking at your own credit report, there will be no negative impact on your credit score. In addition, this is a highly secure, government-run website. You can tell them whatever they want to know—they already know your underwear size anyway and whether you believe that Snowden guy.

However, you choose to get your copy, you will need that complete copy in order to start any disputes. Without it, you will be denied any attention by any of the CRAs and creditors.

Once you have a complete copy of your credit report from all three bureaus, you are ready to begin the process of fixing your own credit!

Be Aware of Imposters

While "AnnualCreditReport.com" is the only legitimate way to pull your credit reports regularly for free, that doesn't mean it is the only site out there offering this service. While these other sites might have offers for free services, they likely come with strings attached, at best, or are simply scams designed to steal your personal information, at worst. Especially be aware of sites whose URLs are misspellings of AnnualCreditReport.com as it is unlikely that they have anything remotely close to benign intentions in mind.

Additionally, you are going to want to keep in mind that AnnualCreditReport.com verifies all of your information directly on the site, which means that if you receive an email claiming to be from this site, then it is likely a form of phishing that is trying to steal your personal information. Likewise, the three major credit reporting agencies never contact individuals directly, which means if you receive a phone call or email from someone claiming to be with either TransUnion, Experian, or Equifax, then the safest choice is just to ignore it.

Chapter 8: Be Familiar with the Credit Bureaus

The best way to manage your credit responsibly is to get the right financial education and know what is best for you. This will take some time and require you to put in the work to learn how everything works. Yet, since your credit scores are so crucial to dealing with your accounts and setting aside cash, you must know as much as you can regarding the credit bureaus that formulate credit appraisals. To assist you with getting started here are key details regarding TransUnion, Experian, and Equifax, the primary credit bureaus of the U.S.:

TransUnion

TransUnion has workplaces nationwide that manage various parts of credit: identity theft, credit management, and other credit issues; and types of credit customers, for example, personal, business, and press inquiries. If you discover errors on your TransUnion credit report, you can call them at 800.916.8800 or visit their site to debate them. If you believe that you are a casualty of identity theft, call them at 800.680.7289 at the earliest opportunity.

Experian

Like other credit bureaus, Experian provides a wide range of various administrations for people, businesses, and the media. Experian is founded in Costa Mesa, CA, and has a website. If you discover errors in your report or need to report potential identity theft, this credit bureau makes it harder to find them through a phone line. Instead, they encourage guests to utilize online forms for questions, identity theft reports, and different issues.

Equifax

Based in Atlanta, GA, Equifax has various departments to help people with multiple types of questions and concerns. Their website is additionally set up to have people utilize online forms to work on errors, report identity theft, and handle different matters. In any case, if somebody believes that their identity has been stolen, the individual in question can call 888.397.3742 to account for it to Equifax. If you detect an error, you can also go through their phone line to get someone that can fix it for you.

These are the three credit bureaus in the nation, and they each adopt different strategies to enable individuals to get in touch with them to pose inquiries or address any issues they might be encountering. Rather than reaching the credit bureaus directly, some people prefer to utilize a credit checking administration to assist them with dealing with their credit and stay on top of their funds. The credit bureaus all have related projects; however, most people prefer to utilize an independent organization to assist them with these issues. That way, they get an impartial perspective on their credit score and a lot more services to manage and improve their credit ratings proactively.

Making the Best of Credit Bureaus

It is important to learn that all three credit bureaus have sensitive financial data. However, there is no method to prevent lenders and collection entities from sharing your information with the above companies. You can limit any possible problems associated with the credit bureaus by evaluating your credit reports annually and acting immediately in case you notice some errors. It is also good to monitor your credit cards and other open credit products to ensure that no one is misusing the accounts. If you have a card that you do not often use, sign up for alerts on that card so that you get notified if any transactions happen, and regularly assess statements for your active tickets. Next, if you notice any signs of fraud or theft, you can choose to place a credit freeze with the three credit bureaus and be diligent in tracking the activity of your credit card in the future.

How the Bureaus Get Their Information

To learn how the score gets calculated, first, we need to learn about all the different inputs of your score, aka where the bureaus get their info. You may have many factors that report information to the credit bureaus or none. Credit cards are called revolving accounts or revolving debt by the credit bureaus. Each month payments and balances are reported, as well as any late payments. This means that any cards that have your name on them will also report to all the bureaus. This includes cards that belong to a spouse or parent. If you are an authorized user on the account, it gets reported on your credit no matter what. Many people have their credit ruined by a spouse or parent going into bankruptcy or not paying their credit card bills. If your name is on any credit card that belongs to people that may not pay their bills, ask them to take your name off immediately! Installment loans also report information to the credit bureaus. If you went down to your local Sears and financed a washer/dryer set by putting up a down payment, that is an installment loan. The details of these loans are all reported; the total balance, as well as the timeliness and amounts of your monthly payments. If you have mortgages or student loans, that information does get reported. Total amounts due, total paid so far, and the status of monthly payments is all reported. This information is kept track of and organized in their databases.

Chapter 9: Check If You Are a Victim of Identity Theft and How to Fix It

Did you ever wonder if people are becoming the perpetrators of identity theft? Or maybe you have been and you're not sure how it happened. There are plenty of approaches used by hackers to get your personal information ahold.

Here we'll explore what identity theft is, how to protect your identity, common identity theft ways, where to turn, and what to do if you're a victim of identity theft, plus how to rebound if it happens to you.

Theft of identity is one form of fraud. It is defined as taking or claiming the identity of another person to use existing accounts, open new credit accounts, or receive other benefits for a fraudulent reason from their personal information. A person's credit cards are usually used for making purchases. Social Security cards and numbers were also taken to establish new credit in your name.

How Identity Theft Happens

Identity theft occurs in a variety of ways; hackers obtain access to your personal information by removing it from your purse or wallet, impersonating an official representative, and accessing your identity through mail and computer technology. Here are some of the conducts identity thieves get your personal data:

Skimming

Occasionally there may be a special storage device connected to the card reader while you swipe your credit card or debit card during a normal transaction. This system collects and stores up to several hundred numbers per credit card at a time. When you transfer the details to a computer, the identity thief will have access to your information without even realizing it.

Hacking

Most identity thieves are also hackers. For businesses that have personal records for the place, they will use smart technology to hack into your personal computers or computer systems. Many banks were also victims of malware and all of their clients may have been victims of identity theft.

Stealing mail

The e-mail provides credit card statements, tax information, bank statements, credit deals pre-approved, and even new checks. Thieves will rob from your mailbox right away and were even known to have mail sent to them. This confidential information is at their disposal and can help them rob their identities.

Dumpster diving

Identity thieves also rummage through your personal garbage, something that often occurs in companies. Robber's search and locate bank account numbers, credit card numbers, financial statements, and other personal information through the trash.

Stealing purses and wallets

Often, identity thieves rummage through your personal trash, something that sometimes occurs in companies. Thieves dig through the garbage and find bank account numbers, credit card numbers, financial statements, and other personal data.

Employees of businesses

Identity thieves can sometimes steal personal records from businesses. This could be an employee's role-taking company documents from his or her own boss in order to gain access to confidential information. Many identity thieves at a business may conspire with an employee who can give them access to personal records. Therefore, workers receiving credit reports can violate their rights to that information.

E-mails and phone calls

Identity hackers were known to impersonate your broker, trustee, or other company representatives by calling or giving you an e-mail. Do not do so if you receive a mysterious phone call or e-mail demanding your personal information to either check your account or to claim the money. They most likely try to steal your credit card number, Social Security number, or other account numbers, whatever the scheme.

Home theft

Many robbers are trying to break into your home not to steal your Television or jewels, but to take your name. They will steal tax information, bank account numbers, Social Security numbers, number of credit card accounts, and any other personal information they might discover.

You might feel robbed, betrayed, and left wondering how this might happen to you. Your credit scores were most likely impacted negatively. You may need a loan or credit, and this condition prohibits you from receiving it. To fix the damage that has already happened and to mitigate potential future harm, you need to take control and figure out what to do next.

Criminal laws regulate identity theft. According to the Identity Theft and Assumption Deterrence Act of 1998 (3. 18 U.S.C. subsection 1028(a) (7)), it is a felony to "consciously pass or use, without legal authority, a means of identifying another person to commit, or aid or abetting, any criminal conduct that constitutes a breach of Federal law or that constitutes a crime under any State or local statute applicable." The law is in place to provide offenders with a consolidated complaint process, as well as improve the criminal laws surrounding identity theft. If you're a victim of identity theft, prompt action is required. The law allows claimants to challenge unauthorized charges; however, some time limits need to be followed.

What to Do If You're a Victim of Identity Theft

Notify the creditor

When you find unauthorized charges on your credit or debit card, then you were most likely a victim of identity theft. The good news is that the Equal Credit Billing Act limits any responsibility for unauthorized charges to $50. When you discover the unauthorized charges, you will have to write down your trustee, disputing the questionable payments.

Write the letter of disagreement to the agency "Billing inquiries" of your creditor. Make sure you send the certified letter to your trustee and you know it's hitting you. Notify the creditor as soon as the unwanted payment is identified and make sure that your letter hits them within 60 days of the first bill revealing the mistake. Keep yourself a copy of the letter. Under statute, the creditor must respond within 30 days of receiving the message, and the conflict must be settled within two billing cycles.

Notify your bank

If your debit card has been stolen, you will report it to your bank within two working days. Under the Electronic Fund Transfer Act, you will only be held liable for $50 in unauthorized charges; however, you will be responsible for $500 of unauthorized charges if you report the unauthorized charges between three and 60 days. Unless you wait until 60 days later, you can lose all of the money stolen from your account. If your debit card has a Visa or MasterCard mark, both firms will limit your liabilities to $50 per card in unauthorized charges.

It's better that you alert your suppliers and banks as soon as you can or your debit cards, credit cards, and even personal checks have been stolen if you detect fraudulent charges. The longer you wait to contact the lender, the greater the chance that some or all of the unauthorized charges will be placed on you.

Fraud alert

If you've been a victim of identity theft, it's important to create a warning about fraud. If you call credit reporting agencies, you will have to choose between two different types of fraud alerts-the expanded warning and the original notice.

The expanded notice entitles you to receive two free credit reports from each credit reporting agency per year; however, for seven years, the fraud alert must stay on your register. The most common type of warning against fraud is the original alarm. This will live 90 days on your file and will send you one free credit report from each of the three reporting agencies.

You have to have a police report and evidence of the theft or attempted fraud to create an extended warning. You may request that for your protection, only the last four digits of your Social Security number appear on your credit report. You may also cancel any warning about fraud at any time.

To set up a fraud alert for your own protection is in your best interest. Creditors will take more precautions when reviewing your credit or loan application and you will be alerted if someone uses your identity to attempt to open accounts. This means the robber can't open credit in your name. You will notify the other credit reporting offices whether you call one of the credit reporting agencies to set up the fraud alert.

Your credit report and credit score are important to you and to your future earnings. Make sure you check them regularly to ensure you're not a victim of identity theft.

Police report

If you suspect that you are a victim of identity theft, it is in your best interests to lodge a police report. Some creditors may require that a police report be used as evidence of the incident. Many police stations hesitate to take a call on identity theft. Assure your submission is permanent. Make sure that you have a copy of the report for your history, because credit card companies and banks may need to see the report and search for unauthorized charges. Remember, make sure that you have the name and phone number of the prosecutor, in case the investors need to talk to him or her.

Social Security Administration

If your Social Security card has been stolen or you know your Social Security number has been used to open new accounts, you will call the Department of Social Security. They will most of the time issue you a new Social Security number and card. To apply for a new Social Security number, you must provide evidence that someone using your account is still harming you. Your sex, U.S. residency, or legal immigration status, and name will need to be confirmed.

Postal inspector

When you believe that your mail was robbed or sent to a different location, you were most likely a victim of identity theft in which a criminal rummaged through your mail or used a Change of Address form to give them your mail. Contact the postal inspector for documentation, and prosecute this fraud.

Department of Motor Vehicles

If you have stolen your driver's license, you need to contact the state agency that issued your license. Most of the time, you can locate their contact information by checking the Department of Motor Vehicles in your state online. They will cancel your license and give you instructions on how to get another license.

Federal Trade Commission

You will report the crime to the Federal Trade Commission (FTC) if you've been a victim of identity theft. Call them at ID THEFT (877), or at www.idtheft.gov. Although the FTC does not prosecute identity theft, it exchanges concerns with local regulatory bodies that support the federal fight against identity theft.

Protecting Yourself from Identity Theft

To deter identity theft from happening to you, it's important that you immediately start taking proactive steps. Additionally, if you've been a victim of identity theft, you must deal quickly with the aftermath to prevent any further harm.

Here are a few of the preventive steps you can take to stop becoming an identity theft victim:

Check your mailbox

You will search the mailbox regularly so that there is no mail left in there for longer than a day or overnight. If your mailbox doesn't have a security feature you should consider getting a lock for your mailbox. Sometimes, consider holding the mail at the post office when you go on vacation so you don't become a victim of identity theft.

Secure your computer

Hackers use smart programming to get what they want from your computer; however, if you are making your computer secure, you can stop them from accessing your private information. Do not store your hard drive financial information, and make sure that your firewall protects your computer. Wireless routers also allow you to create a single password. Make sure you create a password that contains a combination of numbers, characters, and letters. Don't put your passwords on your Mac.

Use a locked file cabinet

Ensure that your financial documents, social security cards, passports, bank statements, credit card statements, and tax information are stored in a locked cabinet or secured safely.

Keeping a list of all your credit cards and account numbers in this secured safe or closed filing cabinet is a good idea. That way, you will have a complete list of account numbers, suppliers, and contact information to dial in an emergency if your wallet or purse ever gets stolen. Do not leave this document outside a locked/secure location anywhere else.

Shred important documents

Do not dispose of your bank accounts, credit card statements, or other financial documents. Thieves have been known to search through the garbage of people seeking personal information that they might use to rob their identity. Instead of throwing away all your important personal records, cover yourself by shredding them. Do not also cut out pre-approved credit card offers, but rip them.

Check credit reports

Checking your credit reports once a year is a wise idea. Under the Equal and Accurate Credit Transactions Act, the three credit reporting agencies can provide you with one free credit report each year.

Chapter 10: Acquire the Right Mindset

Avoiding the Bad Credit with the Right Mindset

A perspective towards money is an overarching mentality you have about your finances. It influences the way you make important financial choices every day.

It will significantly affect your potential to attain your goals. If you shift your perspective on income, you continue to make smarter choices on how problems can be solved.

The influence of constructive thought does indeed apply in this situation.

Features of a Bad Money Mindset

Your attitude towards money is like moral fatigue-it pushes you to act.

If you have a positive mentality about finances, you are more likely to be confident and take the measures you need to take to be effective.

On the other hand, negativity is generating emotions that prevent action:

- Fear or intimidation
- Defeatism
- Procrastination

It's harder to see the way ahead as you shift your attitude towards money and concentrate on the benefits of what you should achieve.

A fresh outlook on money will help you easily reach your goals. So how do you build a positive mentality around money?

Qualities of a Positive Money Mindset

Once you accept financial positivity, you begin to understand that no issue is impossible. This will be done whether you have $5,000 in interest, or $50,000. Your credit score may be 500 but no loan limit would last forever.

When you have a good attitude about your finances, you start searching for possibilities instead of seeing roadblocks and realize that any financial problem is fixable.

The secret to success is to resolve negative feelings, to concentrate on the optimistic.

Employing a positive money mindset to circumvent financial challenges

Positivity may be tough to cultivate while you are in a stressful position, but it is important.

Let's assume you have those above $50,000 credit card debt issues. There are probably several factors that drive your negativity:

- The total monthly contributions are about $1,250 and the budget is close
- But despite spending too much, the balances never seem to drop

- High-interest rates currently make up approximately 60% of every investment you make
- Therefore, if you adhere to the minimal contributions, it would take more than 40 years to recover everything you owe.

The first step to paying off debt and changing your financial behaviors is to adjust the way you think about income. By reflecting on what debt-free life would feel like, gaining financial security, and getting the freedom to invest your money on the stuff you enjoy most, remaining focused and meeting your financial objectives is much simpler.

Your strategic emphasis needs to be on seeking alternatives. You're not the first one to slip into debt so fast. Start from what you know: Minimal payments will not create an impact sufficiently, so you need a better plan. If you just repay the bills at $1,250 instead of meeting the full payment plan the condition changes significantly. It will only take 62 months, instead of 502 months to meet the payout deadline. In reality, five years is a fair amount of time needed for a debt repayment strategy.

Find Financial Balance

Attitude is not the only component of a positive financial mindset. You need harmony too. Stability is what fosters harmony in your financial existence.

When you invest all the energy working on debt retirement, you won't have the money available in case of a disaster. Or if you're wasting the whole day today concentrating on the schedule, you can't properly save for retirement.

A money mantra lets you have a financial target at the forefront of your mind, making taking steps simpler to produce the outcomes you like. Now let's take a peek at how to build a great personal finance mantra.

A Money Mantra

A money motto is a clear statement of what you intend to do in your financial existence. This can either push you to make financially good decisions or discourage you from making poor ones. Its function is to remind you and give you assurance in your everyday life. You state what you wish to manifest, and you are encouraged to behave through the act of having the idea in mind. Start by dreaming about a particular financial target you would like to accomplish during the next six months.

Chapter 11: Take Advantage of the Consumer Credit Laws

The Fair Credit Acts

When you are going about trying to fix your credit, it can often feel as though the deck is stacked against you, however, the truth of the matter is that there are several laws that can help you to even the odds when it comes to dealing with both creditors and credit bureaus.

FCRA

The FCRA does more than just provide you with a free credit report each year, it also regulates the various credit reporting organizations and helps to ensure that the information they gather on you is both accurate and fair. This means that if you see inaccurate information on your credit report, and report it to the relevant agency, they are legally required to look into the matter and resolve it, typically within 30 days. The same applies to agencies or organizations that generally add details to your credit report.

While this won't help you with that particular lender, if the information is inaccurate, you will at least know where to go to clear up the issue. Additionally, if you report an inaccuracy and the credit reporting agency ignores your request you can sue them to recover the damages or a minimum of $2,500. You may also be able to win an additional amount based on punitive damages and legal fees and any other associated costs. You must file legal proceedings within 5 years of when this occurs.

Fair Credit Billing Act

This federal law is part of what is known as the Truth in Lending Act. Its purpose is to provide safeguards to consumers when it comes to unfair billing and make it clear how any errors must be corrected. This law is useful if you are charged for things you didn't purchase, are charged an inaccurate amount for products or services, you didn't receive an item you paid for, payments made aren't reflected in amounts owed, or if your statements are sent to an inaccurate address.

To take advantage of this law, the first thing you need to do is to send a physical letter to the billing inquiries address that the creditor provides. You need to ensure the creditor receives your letter within 60 days from the date the error shows up on your statement. Some creditors allow for disputes to be handled online but utilizing this option can nullify your rights through this law so it is not recommended. The creditor will then have 30 days to acknowledge they received your letter and 90 days to either correct the mistake or tell you why they think it is valid. If they turn down your request you are then allowed to ask for all the documentation saying why they turned you down.

A subset of this law is what is known as the Hidden Gem Law, this means you can dispute any transaction made within 100 miles of your home, or anywhere in your home state, which exceeds $50.

Fair Debt Collection Practices Act

This is another law that benefits consumers when it comes to debt collector actions. This includes not only debt collection agencies but also their attorneys. This law prevents debt collection agencies from contacting you if you have requested that the debt be validated, contacting you instead of your attorney (if applicable) calling before 8 am or after 9 pm, contacting you at work, calling constantly, reporting false information to credit bureaus, embarrassing you in an effort to collect the debt, adding your name to a list of debtors, threatening legal action they can't actually follow through on, misrepresentation or contacting you after you have sent a letter requesting that they stop or saying that you will not pay the debt in question.

If the debt collector breaks these rules or acts in other ways, they are not allowed then you can file a private lawsuit and be recouped costs, fees, and damages. What's more, you don't even need to prove damages and you will likely be awarded a minimum of $1,000.

How The Fair Credit Acts Protect You

The FCRA is a complicated law that bears looking into a little more deeply. Likewise, just because it protects you in a wide variety of ways doesn't mean the credit reporting agency or creditors are always going to follow it the way they should. What follows are several common ways the FCRA is violated on a regular basis.

Reporting Or Furnishing Old Information

While credit bureaus and creditors are required to keep your details as up-to-date as possible, you will frequently find that they fail to do so in several key ways. They will frequently fail to report that a given debt was discharged because bankruptcy was filed, that an old debt is either re-engaged or completely new, report that a closed account is active when it has actually been closed, or keep information that is older than seven years (ten for bankruptcies) on your credit report. If you report these errors, they are legally required to look into them within 30 days.

Reporting Blatantly Inaccurate Information

Creditors are not allowed to provide information to credit bureaus that they know, or should know, is inaccurate. This includes classifying a debt as charged-off when it was really paid in full, altering balances due, reporting a timely payment as late, listing you as the debtor when you were only an authorized user on a specific account, and failing to mention when identity fraud was suspected or confirmed for a given account. Again, if you report these errors, they are legally required to look into them.

Mixing Up Files

While it may seem surprising, credit reporting agencies frequently mix up files on individuals, potentially harming your credit score for someone else's mistakes. These issues can arise between individuals who have similar social security numbers, if you are a Junior or a Senior and the issue is with the other person's credit, mixing up details when names are similar, or even mixing up details for two people with the same zip code.

Violations Of Debt Dispute with Credit Reporting Agencies

Credit reporting agencies have to follow strict rules when it comes to handling disputes; nevertheless, there are frequently issues with the ways they follow through on the process. This includes failing to notify you that a dispute has been received, failing to conduct an investigation into the dispute in a timely fashion, and failing to correct disputes in a timely fashion.

Creditor Debt Dispute Violations

The FCRA also has strict rules when it comes to how creditors must handle disputes, which are frequently disregarded. These violations include things like not notifying credit reporting agencies that a debt is being disputed, not submitting corrected information after the debt has been successfully disputed, not conducting internal investigations into the dispute once they have been notified of the error, making it difficult to submit disputes and not informing you of the results of the investigation into the dispute within five days after it has been completed.

Inaccurate Credit Report Requests

Just because certain individuals are allowed to see your credit report doesn't mean they are allowed to do so at all times. The FCRA ensures that your credit report can't be accessed in order to determine if you are worth filing a lawsuit against, can't be accessed by employers without express permission, and can't be accessed by former creditors related to debts that have been discharged for bankruptcy just to see what your current financial activity is.

Chapter 12: Make Sure to Do Credit Monitoring

In addition to fraud alerts and credit freezes, you can invest in credit monitoring to protect your credit. It means monitoring and inspecting your credit history as shown on your credit report. In the end, that is really what it is all about, your credit report and more importantly unexpected changes to your credit report. A credit monitoring service provides this monitoring service for you (for a fee, of course). Most credit monitoring services report that they monitor and track your credit report daily.

What Happens with Credit Monitoring?

Once you sign up with a credit monitoring company, they pull all your information from all three credit reporting agencies and typically ask if you are in the process of applying for new credit. Often, they will ask you to check the credit report and verify the information. Of course, they will want to know about any activity you consider suspicious. Now, your new credit monitoring service has a baseline or starting point. Any changes to your credit report going forward could be flagged as possibly fraudulent. Depending on the options available and the monitoring plan you chose, you will be alerted to any suspicious activity that could affect your credit report.

The credit monitoring companies typically are on the alert for:

- New credit inquiries
- Delinquencies

- Negative information that suddenly shows up
- Employment changes
- New credit accounts
- Increased credit lines at existing accounts
- Other changes to your credit report that could be considered a red flag for identity theft

You should note that one reason credit monitoring services have become so popular lately is their alerts for suspicious activity on your credit report are viewed as a counter to identity theft. Some credit monitoring companies even promote their services with this claim.

Advantages

- Constant Tracking—All of your credit reports are constantly tracked. Depending on your choice of credit monitoring companies and plans, this monitoring could be daily or weekly.
- Increased Knowledge—about your own credit. During the time you use a credit monitoring service, you will gain an incredibly valuable firsthand knowledge of how personal credit actually works. Simply by watching the reports provided by your credit monitoring service, you will see in real-time how your credit report changes. You will see how even small actions on your part can have a sizeable effect on your credit score. For example, you can watch your credit score drop right after you applied for four different department store credit cards.
- It Does Not Cost, it Saves—Yes, this is a tired old cliché, yet here it truly works. Consider it this way: suppose you use

your new knowledge of how your personal credit works, how small things affect your credit score, and that sort of thing to get a better loan rate. Really, it is that easy. For example, let us say you use your newfound credit wisdom to raise your credit score by 75 points. Then, you refinance your home and get a lower interest rate that saves you hundreds of dollars a month or thousands of dollars over the term of your mortgage.

- Identity Theft Protection—Since your credit report is under constant scrutiny, detection of possible fraudulent activity happens much faster. The credit monitoring service helps you both detect and minimize damage from malicious use of your personal financial information. Additionally, many credit monitoring companies offer legal protections and financial reimbursements. These reimbursements can range from $25,000 to $1,000,000. Surely you have seen the advertisements with the big-name credit monitoring service offering their one-million-dollar guarantee.
- Faster Resolution of Errors—Should you spot an error on one of your many reports sent to you by your credit monitoring service, most of them will assist you in correcting the error.
- No More Guesswork—Since you are paying for professional credit monitoring, you do not have to guess what is going on with your credit score or your credit report. Additionally, since your credit monitoring service will alert you for any suspicious activities, you are always aware of what is happening with your credit.
- Less Hassle for You—Yes, credit monitoring can be done yourself as will be explained shortly. However, paying for a

credit monitoring service eliminates one more thing for you to do.

Disadvantages

- Price—Of course, all of the services provided by credit monitoring companies come at a price. Price is one common complaint against credit monitoring companies. Each company sets its own pricing structure. Also, many of them offer different levels of service at different price points.
- Information Disparity—The information available from one credit monitoring service can be vastly different from another credit monitoring service. Make sure you know what you are paying for when you sign up for a credit monitoring plan.
- Cancellation Issues—There are various reports (complaints) from past customers of some credit monitoring services regarding the difficulty encountered in the service.
- Micromanagement Time Wastes—Because your new credit monitoring service provides you with frequent reports and analyses, you may end up trying to micromanage your credit score. This micromanagement could end up costing you a lot of time with few if any substantive changes to your credit score.
- False Sense of Security—Since you are paying for a credit monitoring service, the tendency is to fall into the trap of that is all you need to do to protect yourself. Identity theft protection involves additional areas beyond your credit report that you still need to monitor.
- A Credit Monitoring Service Cannot do it as Fast as You Might Want—It is not yet possible to monitor a person's credit

history on a real-time basis. For one thing, many creditors only report information on existing clients weekly or even monthly.
- A Credit Monitoring Service is not the Final Solution—Even the very best credit monitoring service is not capable of fully identifying all fraudulent activity. Consider that many credit details are never even reported to a credit reporting agency.

Chapter 13: Get Rid of Your Collection Accounts Once and for All

Collections, as you may already know, is a rather scary subject. But it doesn't have to be. You can get rid of the accounts you have that are in collections and may be utterly ruining your credit score by following the instructions here.

Collections

If you fail to make payments on a particular account, your creditor or lender may decide to sell your account to a debt buyer or send it to a collection agency. This may happen a couple of months after your account becomes delinquent or it may happen when you fail to pay the minimum payment or begin to miss your payments.

This will usually impact your credit score negatively, although each of the credit bureaus uses a different scoring model, so depending on the circumstances the collection account may not affect your score so severely. For instance, an account in collections that had an original debt of fewer than one hundred dollars may be ignored by some of the credit scoring models. Different forms of debt may also be dealt with in different ways. For instance, medical debt may be treated differently from delinquent credit card debt.

Get It in Writing

Let's be clear from the start: whatever you do regarding collections, do it in writing. Do not accept anything that happens merely over the phone or on the internet. Making sure that you send and receive everything related to your collection account by mail is the best way to manage documentation regarding the collection account. And keep a copy of everything you receive in the mail that has to do with your collection account and everything you send.

Also, before you attempt to pay off any debt in collections, you should ask the collection agency to send you proof of what you owe in writing in the form of a debt validation letter. Do not pay until you receive this debt validation letter in the mail. Paying off debt before you receive such a letter can open you up to fraud.

When you send mail regarding your collection account, make a copy, use certified mail, and request a return receipt. This applies all the time, but ESPECIALLY if you do something like send a payment through the mail.

If you call your debt collector in order to negotiate a settlement of your debt, make sure that the collection agency provides you with the terms of that settlement in writing. If you do not have that settlement deal in writing, then even if you pay off the debt according to the terms that were deliberated over the phone, the debt collector can still ask for more money for you, because you do not have any written proof that such a debt settlement payment plan exists. Like we said before, get it in writing!

Note, the one exception to this rule of sending everything in writing is the following. You can make a payment over the internet if the collection agency or debt buyer has a way for you to do so. Make sure that the payment system is secure, and MAKE SURE that you get a receipt for your payment. Once you get a receipt for your payment, print it out and fill it with the rest of your records for that account.

How to Contact

If you suspect that your account has gone into collections but have not yet been contacted by a debt collection agency or a debt buyer, you can try to find out which collection agency your account has gone to by contacting the original lender and asking. Unfortunately, the original lender may not be very helpful in this matter, as it may refuse even to deliberate your account with you since it has already been sent or sold to another agency. You can also try to check your credit report. Remember to check all three credit reports, since the collection account may have been reported to only one or two of the agencies. Also, a brand-new collection account may not show up on your credit report yet.

You can also wait for a phone call or a letter from the debt collection agency and contact them from there. If you get a phone call, be sure to verify its authenticity and the legitimacy of the debt collector by searching for that phone number in a search engine. This will usually help you to determine if the phone call is from a legitimate debt collector or a scammer since the search results will generally provide you with information about past calls from that phone number and what type of call it was.

Don't Do Anything Over the Phone

Like we said before, don't try to do anything over the phone. Or rather, don't put too much stock in any information that is told to you over the phone. And definitely do not try to make a payment over the phone.

Do not accept a phone call as proof that you owe a debt. Find out if the phone number comes from a legitimate debt collector or not. Then, call the debt collector and ask for a written debt validation letter. Do not make any payments until such a letter is in your hands and you have confirmed the authenticity of the debt with it.

As was stated earlier, if you call the debt collector in order to negotiate a settlement of your debt, make sure that the collection agency provides you with the terms of that settlement in writing. If you do not have that settlement deal in writing, then even if you pay off the debt according to the terms that were deliberated over the phone, the debt collector can still ask for more money for you, because you do not have any written proof that such a debt settlement payment plan exists. Like we said before, get it in writing!

Settling Large Collections

In order to settle an account in collections for which you owe a great deal of money, you can do one of the following three things.

You Can Pay Off the Debt as A Lump Sum

The problems caused by your collection account can be quickly resolved if you pay off the amount you owe with one large payment. This may be possible if you receive unexpected or formerly unaccounted-for windfalls such as an inheritance or a tax refund. It may also be possible if you take on some extra work to try to earn money quickly to earn the amount you owe.

Before you do this, make sure it is practical for your circumstances and that using the money to wipe out that large debt will do you better than harm, especially when it comes to the other necessary expenses you must pay.

Be sure to get the lump sum payment agreement in writing before you pay. Also, carefully document your payment and keep receipts and records of the transaction as proof, just in case your payment fails to reach the debt collector or is recorded incorrectly or in case your debt is transferred to another debt collector.

You Can Create a Payment Plan with The Collection Agency to Settle the Debt

If you work with your debt collector to make a payment plan, this can allow you to pay off the debt in a scheduled, manageable, and reasonable fashion. Figure out how much you will be able to afford to pay on a weekly or monthly basis. Call the agency to propose such a payment plan. If the debt collector agrees to your proposal or you negotiate a plan that works for both parties, MAKE SURE that the agency sends you the terms of the deal in writing. Do not pay until you have this written agreement in your hand and you have checked that its terms are correct.

The downside to this is that if you miss any payments, the agreement may be abandoned by the agency, which could attempt to sue for what you owe. This can result in the garnishment of your wages. Also, make sure that the amount you agree to pay is truly within your budget.

You can settle the debt with the debt collector for less than the amount which you owe.

Another way to go is to negotiate a debt settlement for one payment of less than the amount owed. Because collection agencies want to receive some money, they are likely to accept this proposal from you.

The downsides are as follows: Some collection agencies may agree to receive partial payment to settle what you owe, but then they turn around and sell its remaining balance to another collection agency. Also, if the amount forgiven is greater than six hundred dollars, this may be considered taxable income that you will then have to report on your tax return.

If you try to do this, remember: GET IT IN WRITING. If you have the terms of the reduced debt settlement in writing, this will offer you some amount of protection against unscrupulous debt collectors. So, before you make the payment, get the terms of the single payment settlement in writing.

The written agreement from the debt collection agency should state the following. 1. How the agency will report your debt to credit reporting companies. It may be reported as "partial payment" instead of "paid in full," so figure this out before you make an agreement. A "partial payment" in your credit history will still negatively affect your credit score, but it is certainly better for your score than a debt that is wholly unpaid. 2. That the amount you have agreed upon with the debt collection agency is considered sufficient payment for the entirety of your debt.

How to Handle Medical Collections

First, call your health insurance company to make sure that a clerical error hasn't resulted in the huge medical bill you received. Perhaps what you are being charged for is actually covered, but someone reported it incorrectly and you were charged instead as a result. This may be a long shot if your account is already in collections, but it doesn't hurt to try.

Make sure that the bill is accurate and that you are not being charged for any services or care you did not actually receive.

As with normal debt, it is possible to settle a medical debt for less than what you owe. Negotiate with the hospital, the doctor, or the collection agency to see if they will agree to a partial payment of what is owed to settle the debt. As we said earlier, get the terms of the agreement in writing.

If you know that you have medical debt, try to settle it as early as you possibly can, before your account goes into collections. A doctor or a hospital has more motivation to settle a medical debt than a collection agency does.

Will Paying My Collection Accounts Increase My Score?

It depends on the credit scoring model being used. Some scoring models will ignore paid collections, so this will cause your score to improve immediately. For other scoring models, the presence of a collection account on your report (whether paid or unpaid) will continue to have a negative effect until it drops off of your history (which usually happens after seven years). And other scoring models are somewhere in between: your credit score will improve slightly because a collection account marked as "paid in full" will have less of a negative impact than it did when it was unpaid.

Collections: A Step-by-Step Process

Here is an example of the process which will be taken when it comes to collections.

- Step 1—Once your account becomes delinquent, you generally have six months before it gets sent to a debt collection agency. Try to settle your debt while you are still in this phase before it gets sent to collections. Negotiate with your creditor, because your creditor is incentivized to maintain a good relationship with you, the customer.
- Step 2—If you fail to settle your debt before it gets sent to collections, then you will now have to deal with a third-party agency, a collection agency. The debt may still be owned by the original lender, but it is the third-party agency's job to recover some of all of the debt from you, at which point it may earn a commission from your original lender.
- Step 3—The third phase of the debt collection process is when your original lender writes off the debt and sells it (generally for much less than it is worth) to a debt buyer or outside collection agency. Your original lender is, at this point, not involved in the debt anymore. The debt collection agency will still attempt to recover as much of your debt as possible so that it can earn a profit on the purchase of your debt.

Chapter 14: Avoid Foreclosure at All Costs

Foreclosure is one of the most miserable experiences anyone could have in the financial industry. It is usually considered the highest cause of depression in credit operations too. From any perspective anyone might like to view foreclosure, it always ends up becoming a stage no business owner or private individual wants to get.

What is Foreclosure?

What does the term foreclosure mean? To begin with, it has been used to mean all manner of things in different contexts. It depends on whom you ask; a stock trader understands a meaning different from what the security officer understands. It doesn't get any easier if you ask an engineer or a grammarian. They all have what they think it is. In the credit industry none the less, foreclosure is used to describe a situation where the assets of a debtor are sold to clear his debts. That doesn't always happen of course, but a lot of times, this may become necessary in order to clear some, if not all of the debts.

As a practical example, a debtor who takes an auto loan, with the pact that the second he/she is unable to continue paying the debt as outlined in their regulations, the vehicle should be seized and sold to cover the debt left; the business mogul who took some loan and invested in some company's pieces of machinery but end up unable to pay; the traditional who drew a mortgage, courtesy of his company and got fired, became jobless and unable to keep up with his monthly payment, and so many others. Usually, sudden loss of jobs, investments, or expected gains is the reason most people cannot pay up. In order cases, some fall to chronic illness and spend all of their life savings on it, while some others are simply trying to outsmart the credit company. For the last set of people, they suddenly realize there is no way they could keep up with the deal terms because it is choking the life out of them and taking a chunk off their payroll. In any case, they become unable to pay up and their assets stand the risk of being sold to cover up their debts.

More often than not, foreclosure is drawn on debts that are secured. This means the debtor must have added some of his assets as collateral that could be usurped the instant he defaults. They are usually items that can, to a large proportion, cover up the debt. Foreclosure is usually drawn on debts close to close credit too. What's that? The kind of debt drawn on long and well-outlined debts. For instance, credit card debts are not close-credit. There is no specific amount the debtor owes each month, he/she only has the liberty to spend within their credit limit each month, and they may choose to spend or not to. In the close credit case, the precise amount the debtor needs are drafted, the stable payment schedule is drawn and they are expected to turn in some amount at certain periods probably monthly, bi-annually, and so on. That's the kind of plans on which tangible loans like student loans, auto loans, charges mandated by the court, etc. are drawn.

As you would expect, Foreclosure is usually outlined in loan contracts too. It is clearly outlined whether the lender or investor has all the rights to seize the asset the instant the debtor defaults, or there are other clauses to be fulfilled before such assets are usurped. In most cases, lenders are usually individuals or firms who have enough resources to cover up if the debtor defaults, though of course, the debtor is not expected to default. That's why in most cases, creditors involved in this are usually banks or very large credit companies.

Foreclosure isn't simple. It isn't something your creditor can count hours after you default payment and sell off your property. It isn't something your debtor can hope to rope out of without feeling some effects too. The kind of effects and steps taken by both parties is largely dependent on the type of foreclosure drawn. This brings to mind the two types of foreclosure.

The Two Types of Foreclosure

The Judicial Foreclosure

Judicial foreclosure is the type that involves the court before a final resolution is passed on the asset and actions are taken. From my years of experience, debtors often prefer this to the next one we will talk about. But how does this work? The first step is to notify the debtor of his default payments and allow him some time to clear his bill. That grace period is usually according to the earlier agreed terms of deals. If he/she fails to pay up, the lender is expected to proceed to a related court, file a lawsuit called lis pedens against the debtor. Immediately, the case is placed on the public record and the lender is usually allowed to auction off the asset(s).

Non-Judicial Closure

Fairly similar to the former, the non-judicial closure also results in the sale of the asset used as collateral. He/she has been empowered in the deed of the contract. The debtor is sent a note of default before any action is taken; the note is recorded in the county deed's office and the debtor is expected to pay up within a grace period usually between 3-6 months. If they fail to turn in the payment within the grace period, the asset comes directly under the control of the creditor who may choose to auction or reserve it. In most cases, assets are auctioned immediately. If the creditor reserves it, however, the foreclosure deal becomes known as strict foreclosure in some states like Connecticut.

Stages of Foreclosure

By inference, we may point out that there are two basic stages in foreclosure:

The pre-foreclosure stage

The pre-foreclosure is the earliest stage in foreclosure. It is the time between the period the debtor defaults and the time foreclosure happens. It includes the period when a debtor in danger of foreclosure is informed of their debts. The information is usually sent in the form of a note to remind the debtor of how much they are defaulting, and how, according to the rules of the contract they could forfeit some of their resources if they do not pay up. The total amount expected to be paid and the grace period, (the time within which they must pay up) are all found in this note. It foretells what is coming to the debtor. Foreclosure may be averted at this stage if the debtor tries to pay up within the grace period or, in some way, gets the creditors to negotiate a new deal that he/she could comfortably cover. The rule is that credit bureaus are not informed until about 30 days of default, at least, and the record may begin to appear on the credit report after the grace period.

The foreclosure stage

The foreclosure usually happens after the debtor has refused to pay up after the deadline given and has to pay the ultimate decision; let go of his/her asset. The style adopted to gain control of the asset isn't always the same. You will remember that it is defined by the type of foreclosure deal signed. The asset is usually sold within a week, and it is sold at a price usually less than the value of the item, first because the earlier it is cleared off, the earlier the investor got his/her funds. Then, poor upkeep and deterioration may be considered. In cases where the value of the asset has deteriorated so much that the money realized does not cover the total debts or the legal charges incurred in the foreclosure process, the lender may file a claim for a deficiency judgment.

What to Do When You Default?

Strike a new deal

Foreclosure can have a drastic effect on your credit card, and that's exactly why it may become necessary to involve every means possible. In many cases, it is realistic to open a new negotiation with your creditor. Let them see reasons you cannot afford to pay right now and propose infallible, and favorable alternatives. It's saved millions of people.

Right of redemption

The statutory right of redemption is a law that states that after a debtor has defaulted and the lender or creditor has taken control of their resources, the debtor may reclaim this asset. This may happen even if the lender has auctioned off the asset, as long as the redemption is done within the redemption period which is the period left for the defaulter to pay. Of course, that sounds weird for someone who hasn't paid the debt he/she owes, and that's why some terms must be in place.

In the first case, a debtor may reclaim his property if they pay up the precise amount they owe and the legal charges incurred in the foreclosure process. They may also retain their home if they participate in the auctioning which is usually announced on local radios for a fixed date, and then make the highest bid which gives them control again. If the cost of the house covers the debt incurred, the debtor would be permitted to own the house, but if they have more to pay, they would likely be served a deficiency judgment and would have to pay more. In most cases, debtors may make a profit by reselling the asset for a higher price, and they may pay off their debts with the profit. In the last case, a debtor may declare bankruptcy.

Declare bankruptcy

Declaring bankruptcy is the final resolution for anyone who can't afford their debt and is worried about losing their property. Often, people obtain secured loans using their most valuable resources such as houses or cars as collateral. When they eventually realize they cannot pay up, they may resort to declaring bankruptcy. How does that help? They may retain control of the asset if the asset is considered one of the basic assets that cannot be lost in bankruptcy. Usually, that includes cars and basic company facilities. Notwithstanding, I must be quick to add that bankruptcy is the worst record on your credit profile.

You must be wondering by now; how bad can a foreclosure be on your profile? What harm can it do, if any? I am going to talk about that now:

Effects of Foreclosure on Credit Scores

Poor Credit Scores

We may outrightly begin with this. The most drastic effect that your foreclosure may cause on your credit report is poor credit scores. According to FICO's reports in 2019, you may witness a fall between 185 to 105 in your credit scores if you go through a foreclosure. There are speculations that the better your current scores, the more you feel the direct effects of foreclosure. Practically, you have just shown that sometimes, you do not even have the means to continue payment and your creditors might have to engage in property sales to get their money. Of course, you don't mean it that way. You did it because finances were tough and your creditors have to be paid, but it is the only way other creditors and potential lenders can read it.

You Risk an Awful Record on Your Profile

Having an awful record on your profile is a stigma you'd have to bear for quite a long while. By FRCA regulations, poor records such as bankruptcy, foreclosure, short sales are likely to remain in your credit record for a long time. By this, I mean until the next seven years at least, your credit report will bear that you have suffered a financial imbroglio at some point, that got so tough you had to give up some of the things you had, and that it may likely repeat itself. In the first place, it is hard to regain better credit scores, and you might have to spend a couple of years trying, at least. It is more difficult to erase this record even when you have better grades. It is boldly in the section where your public judgments are expected and you can attempt its removal until 7 years after.

Higher Charges for Conventional Financing

Now, this is one other problem. There are high chances that it will become pretty hard for you to get what others get easily. Lenders become unsure about your payment capacity, no matter what you present. They always want some cynical way to be assured. That is probably why you would be charged a higher interest rate when every other person. This might make it unbearable to obtain a lot of loans and you have to brace yourself up for that.

Getting A New Loan Becomes Hard

You may regard this as the full implication of forfeiture. It usually leaves a bad impression, and it makes it practically impossible to get a new loan without stringent clauses or conditions. It is either that you need to pay higher interest or you need to put down some deposits higher than others do. You may also be required to fill forms that you otherwise wouldn't, but all that is if you are not turned down.

So, you see, you must carefully consider your options before watching foreclosure happen. Particularly if you are at the pre-foreclosure stage. The long-term effects are drastic and it may become too difficult to wipe off. You have every chance to avert it and it is always recommended that you try to stop it from happening.

Conclusion

So far, in the journey of your credit repair, you have been exposed to a series of ideas, concepts, and strategies you need to carry out to make your life better. It is no more news that your credit score affects your life all around, even in ways that you never imagined. It could be a roadblock to opportunities that could change your life forever. At the same time, could be the access point to the good life you have always hoped for.

This is the most foundational truth that credit repair companies do not want you to realize. It is true that the process involves some technicality and therefore requires some measure of tactics to see through, but this is not to say you cannot do it all by yourself with the right information. It is highly advisable to personally address your credit issues to keep you informed on the basic areas where you need to pay more attention to your day-to-day transactions.

More often than not, using credit cards both for small and big purchases causes trouble for most people. The most common reason is missing payments promptly, which may be due to oversight, financial emergencies, or a tight financial state.

As you have learned from this book, you need to obtain a copy of your credit report.

Once you have a copy of your credit history, examine it thoroughly. It is best if you compare each item with your stubs of payments and spending. For any inaccuracy, mistake, or discrepancy, make sure to contact the concerned credit bureau and request for an investigation on the item in question. Make sure to request the investigation once you have found out about the inaccuracy so that you can take action immediately and proceed to repair your credit. It is also advisable to establish a timeline once you have requested an investigation from the credit bureau. Check with the agency again if they fail to respond within your timeline or 30 days. If the credit agency does not return within 30 days, request for the removal of the item in question from your credit report. Again, it is your right to have it removed due to non-compliance with the agency.

On the other hand, if there is no inaccuracy in your report and you admit that your bad credit situation is your own doing, you should seriously monitor your finances. Make sure to plan your finances. For instance, cut down on unnecessary spending and pay your creditor the full amount due. Most creditors provide their customers with additional time to pay up debts; however, it would only add up to your expenses if you delay your payment.

When you are dealing with a creditor, it is best to let them know that you are serious about repairing your credit. More often than not, creditors appreciate the effort of their customers in repaying their debts as it saves both time and effort. However, make sure that whatever deal you come up with, you would stick to your word.

The process of credit repair is a circumstance from which you can learn. For instance, you would learn to use your credit wisely once you obtain a good credit rating given that you would not want to go through the entire credit repair process again. You also learn to control your spending urges, specifically those transpiring at the spur of the moment. Finally, you learn how important it is to keep copies of your credit card and pay stubs.

Once you have done that, the next step is to go through each credit report from the credit bureau ensuring to check or ascertain the accuracy of all entries to ensure that they are correctly stated.

If anything is not stated, as it should find which strategy could work best for your situation, then follow that method to dispute any derogatory items from your credit report. As you do that, don't give up easily; the credit bureaus pry on people like you who give up on their rights. Even as you continue disputing derogatory items from your credit report, you need to study the relevant laws to ensure that you can use the law to your benefit even to get more derogatory items removed from your credit report.

I hope you have learned something!

BOOK 3
609 LETTER TEMPLATES & CREDIT REPAIR SECRETS

Discover All the Hacks the Experts Don't Share About Dispute Letters and Boost Your FICO Score by Over 200 Points in Less Than 30 Days at No Cost

Introduction

A 609 is known as a dispute letter, which you would send to your creditor if you saw you were overcharged or unfairly charged. Most people use a 609 letter in order to get the information they feel they should have received. There are several reasons why some information might be kept from you.

A section 609 letter is sent after two main steps. First, you see that the dispute is on your credit report. Second, you have already filed and processed a debt validation letter. The basis of the letter is that you will use it to take unfair charges off your credit report, which will then increase your credit score.

The 609 letters can easily help you delete your bad credit. Other than this, there are a couple of other benefits you will receive from the letter. One of these benefits is that you will obtain your documentation and information as the credit bureau has to release this information to you. Secondly, you will be able to obtain an accurate credit report, which can definitely help you increase your credit score.

There are also disadvantages to the 609 letters. One of these disadvantages is that collection agencies can add information to your credit history at any time. A second disadvantage is that you still have to repay debt. You cannot use the 609 letters to remove the debt that you are obligated to pay. Finally, your creditor can do their investigation and add the information back into your credit report, even if it was removed (Irby, 2019).

One of the reasons section 609 came to be is because one of five people state that they have inaccurate information on the credit report (Black, 2019). At the same time, many people believe that this statistic is actually higher than 20 percent of Americans.

How to File a Dispute with Section 609

You should make sure all the procedure is done correctly, as this will make it more likely that the information will come off and no one will place it back on your report again.

- Make the necessary changes to the letter. This will include changing the name and address. You must also make sure your phone number is included. Sometimes people include their email address, but this is not necessary. In fact, it is always safer to only include your home address or PO Box information. You must also check the whole letter. If something does not match what you want to say, such as what you are trying to dispute on your credit report, you need to state this. These letters are quite generic, which means you need to add in your information.
- Make sure that all of your account information you want to be taken off your credit report is handwritten. Likewise, we recommend you use blue ink rather than black. On top of this, you do not need to worry about being too neat, but make sure they can read the letters and numbers correctly. This is an important part of filing your dispute letter because handwritten ones in blue ink will not be pushed through their automated system. They have an automatic system that will read the letter for them and punch in the account

number you use. They will then send you a generic letter that states these accounts are now off your credit report, which does not mean that it actually happened. When you write the information down, a person needs to read it and will typically take care of it.
- You must prove who you are with your letters. While this is never a comfortable thing to do, you must send a copy of your social security card and your driver's license or they will shred your letter. You also need to make sure that you get each of your letters notarized.
- First, you could damage their reputation, and secondly, you will cost them more money than simply taking the information off your credit report will.
- It is necessary to keep all correspondence they send you. You should also wait at least three months and then re-run your credit report to make sure the wrong information has been removed. Keep track of every time you need to re-run your credit report as you can use this as proof if they continue to send you a letter stating the information is off of your credit report.

What Are My Rights Under 609?

This agency is going to list all of the responsibilities that credit reporting companies and any credit bureaus will have, and it includes the rights of the consumer that will be your rights in this situation.

When using this act, the consumer has to be told if any of the information on your file has been in the past or is now being used against you in any way, shape, or form. You have a right to know whether the information is harming you and what that information is.

This Act is going to limit the access that third parties can have to your file. You personally have to go through and provide your consent before someone is able to go through and look at your credit score, whether it is a potential employer or another institution providing you with funding.

Chapter 1: What is Section 609?

Section 609

The first thing that we need to take a look at here when it comes to our credit scores is what Section 609 is really all about.

For example, when we are using this Act, the consumer has to be told if any of the information that is on your file has been in the past, or is now being used against you in any way, shape, or form. You have a right to know whether the information is harming you, and what that information is.

In addition, the consumer is going to have the right to go through and dispute any information that may be seen as inaccurate or incomplete at the time. If they see that there are items in the documents they are sent, if the billing to them is not right or there is something else off in the process, the consumer has the right to dispute this and the credit reporting agency needs to at least look into it and determine if the consumer is right.

Other issues that are addressed in this Act are going to be done in a manner that is the most favorable to the consumer. This Act is going to limit the access that third-parties can have to your file. You personally have to go through and provide your consent before someone is able to go through and look at your credit score, whether it is a potential employer or another institution providing you with funding.

They are not able to get in and just look at it. Keep in mind that if you do not agree for them to take a look at the information, it is going to likely result in you not getting the funding that you want, because there are very few ways that the institution can fairly assess the risk that you pose to them in terms of creditworthiness.

Along with some of the other parts that we have discussed above, the consumer does have the option to go out and seek damages from those who violate the FCRA if they can prove that it happened.

Another thing to note about all of this is that the FCRA is going to be divided into sections. And each of these sections is going to come with a unique set of rules that all credit bureaus need to follow. In particular, section 609 of the FCRA is going to deal with disclosure and is going to put all of the burdens of providing the right kind of documentation on the credit bureaus.

You do not have to come up with a way of proving whether or not the item on the credit report is legitimate or not. Instead, that is up to the credit bureaus. And there are many cases where they are not able to do this. Whether they brought the debt and did not have the proper documentation, or there is something else that is wrong with it, the credit company may not be able to prove that you are the owner of it or that you owe on it at all. If this is the case, they have to remove the information from your credit report. When a bad debt is taken off, or even a collection is taken off, that does nothing but a lot of good for your overall score.

We are going to take some more time in this section to look over Section 609 from the FCRA. But this is the basics of what you need to know.

Why Use a 609 Letter?

The 609 Letter is going to be one of the newest credit repair secrets that will help you to remove a lot of information on your credit report, all of the false information, and sometimes even the accurate information, thanks to a little loophole that is found in our credit reporting laws.

You can use this kind of letter to resolve some of the inaccuracies that show up, to dispute your errors, and to handle some of the other items that could inaccurately come in and impact and lower your credit score.

When it is time to report your credit history at all, one of the credit bureaus is going to be responsible not only to include information that is verifiable but also accurate in the report. The use of this letter in credit repair is going to be based mostly on the idea of whether the credit bureau was responsible for how they verified the information they put onto the report and if they can do it on time.

Credit bureaus are going to collect information on consumer credit from a lot of different sources like banks, and then they are going to be able to resell that information to any business that would like to evaluate the consumer credit applications. Credit bureaus are going to be governed by the FCRA or the Fair Credit Reporting Act, which is going to help detail what credit reporting agencies and information furnishers can, and can't, do when they decide to report information on the consumer.

Using these 609 letters is a good way for us to clean up our credit a bit, and in some cases, it is going to make a perfect situation. However, we have to remember that outside of some of the obvious benefits that we are going to discuss, there are a few things that we need to be aware of ahead of time.

Few limitations are going to come with this as well. For example, even after you work with the 609 letters, it is possible that information that is later seen as accurate could be added to the report again, even after the removal. This is going to happen if the creditor, after the fact, is able to verify the accuracy. They may take it off for a bit if the 30 days have passed, and they are not able to verify at that point. But if the information is accurate, remember that it could end up back on the report.

New debt collection agencies could go through and add some more outstanding debts to your credit report at any time. This could bring the score back down, especially if you are not careful about how you spend your money and handle debts along the way.

While some people think that it is possible, keep in mind that you are not able to eliminate any obligations to repay a legitimate debt. Even if you write out a 609 letter and you are able to get that debt removed from the credit report, whether that is for the short term or the longer term, you still have to pay that legitimate debt. Don't use this as a way to hide from your debts or get away from paying them at all. Use this as a method that will help you to clear out some of the older options, or some of the debts that you have taken care of, but still remain on your reports.

In addition, contrary to some of the myths that are out there when it comes to these 609 letters, the FCRA is not going to require that any of the credit agencies keep or provide signed contracts or proof of debts.

The FCRA, though, is going to give you as a consumer the right to go through and dispute some of the errors that show up on your credit report. This is not a way for you to go through and make some of your student loans or other debts go away, so you don't have to pay them any longer. But it is going to be one of the best ways that you are able to get information that is not accurately taken off the credit report.

We are able to get a lot of things done when we work with the Section 609 letters, but they are not a magic pill that will make things disappear for us. They will make it easier for us to go through and get rid of information that is not correct and can ensure that we can get rid of debts that maybe we settled in the past, but are still harming our credit. This is going to make it easier overall for us to really ensure that we can get things organized and get the higher credit score that we are looking for.

Chapter 2: How to Open a Dispute

So, now that you have determined that there are areas of your credit report that contain erroneous information, you want to file a section 609-letter seeking redress. However, you are probably wondering if there are any steps to take to ensure that your letter is received and acted on as quickly as possible. Filing a section 609 letter like any other process has certain guidelines that will help your letter receive the attention you desire and increase your chances of getting erroneous information removed from your report.

One of the most important things to keep in mind when filing a section 609 letter is that a section 609 letter does not necessarily let you dispute whatever claim it is you have an issue with on your credit report. This is particularly important because it is a distinction which a lot of people do not get and one, they pay dearly for when their letters go unattended by the credit reporting agency.

The essence of a section 609 letter is to challenge records entered into your credit report by your credit reporting agency. With a section 609 letter, you can request that the documents behind any entry on your credit report be made available to you. This process is not a surefire way to getting an item removed from your credit report.

However, it is a helpful procedure as it requires the credit reporting agency to provide some information that can be difficult to procure about the fishy item on your credit report. The section 609 letters might not be a guarantee that an item will be expunged from your credit report, but it is your right under the FCRA, and you should not hesitate to use it if you feel you need to.

Some Helpful Steps for Writing a Section 609 Letter

The section 609 letters might not be a guaranteed way to remove an item from your credit report, but it is worth the effort to try to remove something with a section 609 letter.

1. Make Sure to Establish Your Identity

Now, there are a couple of informal guidelines to remember when handling a section 609 dispute, but the first and perhaps most important thing to remember is that you need to have impeccable documentation attached to your letter.

So, you must include documents establishing your identity in your section 609 letters. Some documents that you can include are:

- A birth certificate
- A driver's license
- Your social security number
- A copy of the credit report with your account highlighted

These documents are not the only ones that can be included, however. Practically any document that can help to establish your identity can be included with the section 609 letters. It does not really matter whether that document is a rent agreement or a utility bill; just make sure to identify yourself beyond any doubt. Be careful to make sure that you do not send in the original copies of any of your documents for identification due to the risks associated with that. Make photocopies of all the necessary documents and send in the photocopies instead of the originals.

If you deliver your section 609-letter using the mail, you should make sure to save the delivery receipt so that you can keep track of when your mail is delivered to the credit reporting agency. The reason why you should keep the delivery receipt is so that you are able to monitor the delivery time of the letter and be sure when it arrives at the credit reporting agency.

Section 609 of the FRCA act stipulates that the credit reporting agency must respond to your query within 30 days. If you are able to track when your letter arrives, you can calculate the timeframe within which the credit reporting agency is supposed to reply, and if you do not receive a reply within that period, you can legally demand that the record be removed from your credit report.

2. Be Very Exact About Your Claim

Now that you have made sure that there is proper documentation, you need to make sure you do not go around in circles when writing your section 609 letters. Don't be vague about the claim you are trying to dispute, be exact, state the claim clearly. Any vagueness in your letter can be enough reason for your letter to be ignored as the claim you are attempting to dispute cannot be ascertained.

When you have clearly stated the reason for your letter, then you must also go ahead and specifically ask that the credit reporting agency specifically looks into the issue you have raised. Also, make sure to politely request a reply from the credit reporting agency, either expunging the error from your credit report or, if there is nothing wrong, that they provide proof that nothing is wrong. In order to make sure you are precise about your claim, you can follow a format like this when writing your letter:

"I am writing to request that information concerning (report) which is on my credit report (account number). I would like to see the original source of this information which I believe is found on the original contract I signed with your agency."

3. Be Careful How You Word Your Letter

Even if you are certain that you have a legitimate dispute that you are addressing with your section 609 letters, you should still be careful not to come across as someone who is looking to pick a fight or quarrel with the credit reporting agency. You must find a way to strike a balance between being polite and being firm.

You must also be concise; a section 609 letter is not really supposed to be very long or very wordy; as such three brief paragraphs should be enough for you to identify yourself, state your claim, and point to the documentation you have provided. Considering that the credit reporting agency probably has no vendetta against you and that it is humans who will be tasked with processing your letter, it is important to come across with as much decorum as possible.

Some Other Things to Consider

However, there is a lot of information currently flying around about section 609 letters which is unverifiable and misleading; there are also a few general things to do or not do as it concerns section 609 letters.

- Don't send a section 609 letter without making sure that the claim you are disputing is verifiably erroneous. The section 609 letter is not a silver bullet that will magically remove a claim from your credit report and fix your credit rating score, contrary to what most people say on the internet. Be absolutely certain that the claim you are requesting information for is really erroneous. Now granted, there is some margin for error here, but try and be as certain about the claim you are making as you can possibly be.

- Don't send section 609 letters frequently for no reason. When they are not making it sound like a silver bullet to fix your problems, most people are making the section 609 letters feel like a lottery. However, it is simply not true that sending in more letters increases your chances of getting anything fixed. The section 609 letter is basically a letter of request. The credit reporting agency will look into your claim and provide the requested documentation, and if they are not available, the erroneous information will simply be removed from your credit report, that's all.
- Do not bother too much about a section 609-letter template. A whole business niche has sprung up around selling section 609 letter templates, with some of them guaranteed to give you higher chances of getting the disputed claim removed from your credit report. If you are going to buy a letter template, let it simply be because you want the extra convenience of not having to draft out the letter yourself.
- Keep a record of every document you send to the credit reporting agency as part of your section 609-dispute letter. Be sure to make photocopies of documents before sending them in and to file all the related documents in a folder chronologically so that you are able to independently

establish a timeline of events in your attempt to get your credit report fixed.
- If you feel overwhelmed by the process, simply do not have the time, or just want to outsource your 609-letter filing and related activities, do not hesitate to make use of a credit repair agency.
- All things being equal, the section 609 letter does offer a viable path to raising your credit score if there are problematic claims on your credit report. So, don't hesitate to get started on the process of sending in a section 609 letter. Follow the steps we have outlined, send in your section 609 letters, and hopefully, you will get a favorable reply in no time.

Chapter 3: Tips to Have Success with 609

While you might not care to do this when it comes to the credit bureau, they often pay more attention to letters that are done professionally. Furthermore, many letters are placed to the side because the customer did not include all the information or correct documentation.

These are not only tips detailing the information you should put into your dispute letter, but they are also tipping from people who have successfully used the 609 loopholes to repair their credit.

Include Documentation

When it comes to your dispute letter, it is important to remember that documentation is key. First, this makes your case that what is written on your credit report is wrong. Even though the credit bureau still has up to 90 days to investigate your claims, making sure to send the documentation is going to result in your case being even stronger. Furthermore, it proves that you completely understand what this wrong information is doing to your credit report and that you intend to fix this, which is your right provided by section 609.

You want to include as much documentation as you need to. This means that you can send a copy of your credit report, including highlighting the wrong information. At the same time, you need to make sure that the information is also handwritten in your letter. Enclosing a copy of your credit reports simply proves that this information is truly on your report and is not made up.

You also want to make sure that you include the information to verify that you really are yourself. If copies of your identification card, such as a state-issued ID or driver's license along with your social security card are not enclosed, they might not take any action with your letter. The fact is that this letter could have been written and sent by anyone.

You also want to make sure that you send any copies of checks, credit card receipts, and any correspondence. This means that if you are sending your second letter to the credit bureau, you should also include your first letter.

Never send originals to the credit bureau. You always want to make sure that you send copies and keep the originals for yourself.

Be Thorough

This might mean that you spend a good amount of time writing your letter. You must keep it about a page in length, make sure that everything is readable, and you do not make the print too small. The best font to use is Times New Roman and the best size to use is 12-point font. This is standard when it comes to business letters. You do not need to pick the fun font as this is not meant to be a fun and interesting letter; it is meant to be straight to the point and to provide all the information necessary.

The trick is to simply state the facts, such as what is wrong and what you want to happen so the issue is resolved. You do not really need to explain why you think it is wrong, but you need to explain what the situation is.

Illustrate Your Case

You want to make sure that you explain what about the information you believe to be wrong. You do not just want to say that certain information on your credit report is wrong and you would like it removed and then list the incorrect information. You want to make sure that you give them information that makes you prove it is wrong in a written way. You will want to give them the numbers for the incorrect information, which will be shown on your credit report, and then move on to the other item or finish the letter. You will then want to include documentation proving that you made these payments.

Proofread the Letter Thoroughly

You do not want to be in so much of a hurry to send this letter that you spell something incorrectly.

It is important to not just read the words but also to make sure all the numbers are correct.

Proofreading your letter will also help you make sure that you have all the necessary information but did not become too detailed.

Get Advice If Necessary

If you want to make sure that you are reading your credit report correctly or you want to get reassurance that you are correct, you can seek advice from a professional. You do not have to contact an attorney; you can simply go to your financial advisor or someone else you trust for help. For example, loan advisors at banks regularly read credit reports and might be willing to help you, especially if you have a relationship with the banker.

Of course, there is also a lot of advice that you can find online. There are a lot of people who share their stories of writing letters and are willing to help you with anything you need to make sure that you get all incorrect information taken off your report.

What Not to Disclose in Your Letter

It is just as important to make sure that you do not disclose certain information.

First, you never want to disclose what you do not want to dispute. This means that you do not want to write anything in your letter that is correct on your credit report. Some people will often scan their credit report and blackout the other information that the credit bureau does not need to see with the letter. They might do this in order to highlight what is wrong or for their own protection.

Secondly, unless you have a legitimate reason to do so and you have gotten advice from an attorney, you do not want to threaten legal action. This can be okay to do by the time you are sending your third letter. However, you always want to make sure to get legal advice before you threaten to sue anyone. This is just an extra step to make sure that you do not cross any legal lines that you are unaware of.

Third, you do not want to dispute any credit card payments that you fell behind on recently.

Finally, there are ways that you can dispute over the phone or online. However, it is advised that you never do this. One of the main reasons you do not want to do this is you are not allowed to keep copies of correspondence. While you never want to end up going to court over this claim, and this rarely happens, you always want to act like this could happen. Another reason is that when you try to dispute over the phone, you need to verbally agree to certain terms. These are often stated in a very confusing way. One of the most common agreements made over the phone that you would never agree to on paper is to waive any right to a reinvestigation. This means that if the credit bureau states nothing could be found to support your claim, you cannot try to reopen the case. In general, disputing online or over the phone is a huge disadvantage for you.

Make Sure Everything Is Readable

No matter what you send, you want to make sure that someone else will be able to read it. This is another reason why someone having proofread your letter is often the best option as they will be able to tell you if something is not readable or does not make sense.

While you should do your best to type as much information as possible, you should not write the letter by hand. While this will be accepted, it is generally not something that people do in this day and age. Furthermore, typing most of the information will ensure that words are not mistaken for another word, which can happen with handwriting. While you might feel your handwriting is easily readable, someone else might not be able to understand it as well.

Do not Bypass the Credit Reporting Agency

Some people feel that having to write a dispute letter to the credit bureau is a long road. Instead, they want to direct it to the lender. This is a common mistake that people make and one that can make the process longer than it initially is.

Another reason people often go directly to the lender is that section 609 states that you can do this. However, this also makes it, so you have more difficulty fighting your case. Chances are that the lender is not going to fix the mistake very easily. If you find that you need to take stronger measures, you could have a bigger struggle on your hands because you did not contact the credit bureau first.

Chapter 4: What Next? How to Proceed with the Letters?

Now that we know a little bit more about Section 609 and how we can use this for some of our own needs when it is time to handle our credit report and get the different parts to increase, it is time to look at how we can proceed with these letters. In the following section, we are going to take a look at the steps that you can utilize to write out one of these Section 609 letters. But then it is time to figure out what we want to do with them when the letter is written. There are a few different ways that we can make sure these letters get back to the right parties, and all of them are listed below:

Emails

Our world seems to run online and using this we can find ways to work on our credit scores. Not having to waste a lot of time copying things or worrying about the paper trails can seem like a great idea, and in some cases, we may find that sending in our 609 letters through email is going to be the best situation for our needs.

Before you do this, though, make sure that you take the time to do the proper research. You want the forms to end up in the right locations, rather than getting sent to the wrong departments and not doing anything for you in the process. Most of the time there will be listings for the various departments that you want to handle and work with for each credit agency, so take a look at those.

Again, when you are ready, you need to have as many details as possible ready to go for this. Just sending in a few lines about the process and thinking that will get things done is foolish. Write out a letter just like you would if you planned to send these by mail and use that as the main body of your email. Mention Section 609 and some of the disputes that you want to bring up.

In addition to this, you need to take some time to add in the other details. Attach some ways to prove your identity to the email, along with a copy of the credit report that has been highlighted to show what is going on and what you would like to dispute. Add in any of the other documentation that is needed to help support your case and have it as cleaned and organized as possible to make sure the right people can find it and will utilize this information to help you out.

Doing it All Online

Many of the credit agencies have made it easier to go through and work on some of these claims online. This helps you out because you will not need to go through and print it all or worry about finding the paperwork and printing a bunch of things. Also, if you are already on your credit report, your identification has been taken care of.

Don't take the easy way out of this. If you just click on the part that you think is wrong and submit a claim on it, it won't be enough. There won't be any reference back to Section 609, and you will not be able to get them to follow the rules that come with Section 609 necessarily.

This is where being detailed is going to be useful in the long run. When you do submit one of these claims online, make sure that you write a note with it to talk about Section 609, specifically the part of 609 that you want to reference in this dispute.

You can usually attach other forms to document who you are, and why you think the errors need to be dropped.

Treat this just like you would if you tried to mail the information to the credit agency.

Telephone

A telephone is one method that you can use, but it is not usually the right one for this kind of process. For example, how easy is it going to be to show the credit agency what your driver's license looks like? You can repeat the number over if you would like, but this process is still a bit more laborious than some of the others and doesn't always work as well as we hope it would.

However, this is an option that we can use to reach the credit agencies, and for some people who are not sure of what their rights are, or would rather talk directly to the individuals in charge about this issue, the telephone can be the right option. Make sure that you have a copy of your credit report in front of you when you start and having some other identification information and more.

Just like we will show when working on our letter templates, later on, we need to make sure that we speak about the issue at hand, explain our rights, and go through the information on Section 609. There is the possibility that the other side is going to have some questions for you, and they will at least want to go through and verify your identity to make sure they are ready to go. But the same rules apply here, and if you don't get a response within 30 days of that phone call, then the information should be erased.

Keep a record of what is discussed in that conversation, who you talked to during that time, what time and date it was, and so on. This will make it easier to get someone to respond to you and can help us get this to work in our favor.

Mail

Another option that you can work with is mail. This is usually a good method to use because it allows you a way to send in all of the information at once. Since you probably already have a physical copy of your SSN, driver's license, credit report, and more, you can get copies of these made pretty quickly, and then send them along with the Section 609 letter. This method also allows us a way to go through and circle or highlight the parts of our credit report that we want to point out to the credit reporting agency.

This method is quick and efficient and will make sure that the information gets to the right party. You can try some of the other options, but sometimes this brings up issues like your information getting lost in the spam folder or getting sent to the wrong part. Mails can take some of that out of the way and will ensure that everything gets to the right location at the right time.

Certified Mail

For the most part, you are going to find that working with a certified mail is going to be one of the best options that you can choose. This will ensure that the letter gets to the right place and can tell you for certain when the 30-day countdown is going to begin.

If you send this by regular mail, you have to make some guesses on when the letter will arrive at the end address that you want, and sometimes you will be wrong. If there is a delay in the mailing and it gets there too late, then you may start your 30 days too early. On the other hand, if you assume it is going to take so many days and it takes less, you may wait around too long and miss your chance to take this loophole and use it to your advantage.

A certified mail can fix this issue. When the credit agency receives the letter, you will get a receipt about that exact date and even the time. This is going to make it so much easier for you since you can add these to your records. There is no guessing along the way, and you can be sure that this particular loophole is going to work to your advantage.

Another benefit that comes with certified mail is that you make sure that it gets to its location. If you never get a receipt back or get something back that says the letter was rejected or not left at the right place, then you will know about this ahead of time. On the other hand, if it does get to its location, you will know this and have proof of it for later use.

Sometimes things get lost, but you want to be on the winning side of that one. If the credit agency says that they did not receive the letter, you will have proof that you sent it and that someone within the business received it and signed for it. Whether the company lost it along the way, or they are trying to be nefarious and not fix the issue for you, the certified mail will help you get it all to work for you.

When it comes to worrying about those 30 days and how it will affect you, having it all in writing with receipts to show what you have done can take out some of the guesswork in the process. This will ensure that you are going to get things to work for you if the 30 days have come and gone, and no one will be able to come back and say that you didn't follow the right procedures.

As we can see, there are a few different options that we can use when it comes to sending out our Section 609 letters.

Chapter 5: 12 Templates of 609 Letter

Letter #1: Initial Letter to Credit Bureau Disputing Items

{Name of Bureau}

{Address}

{Date}

{Name on account}

{Report number}

To whom it may concern:

On {Date of Credit Report} I received a copy of my credit report which contains errors that are damaging to my credit score. I am requesting the following items be completely investigated as each account contains several mistakes.

{Creditor 1 / Account number}

{Creditor 2 / Account number}

{Creditor 3 / Account number}

Thank you in advance for your time. I understand that you need to check with the original creditors on these accounts and that you will make sure every detail is accurate. I also understand that under the Fair Credit Reporting Act you will need to complete your investigation within 30 days of receiving this letter. Once you are finished with your investigation, please send me a copy of my new credit report showing the changes. Looking forward to hearing from you as I am actively looking for a new job and wouldn't want these mistakes on my credit report to stand in my way.

Sincerely,

{Your signature}

{Your Printed Name}

{Your Address}

{Your Phone Number}

{Your Social Security Number}

Attach a copy of the credit report showing which accounts you are disputing

Letter #2: When You Don't Get a Response from Letter #1

{Name of Bureau}

{Address}

{Date}

{Name on account}

{Report number}

To whom it may concern:

On {Date of your first letter} I sent you a letter asking you to investigate several mistakes on my credit report. I've included a copy of my first letter and a copy of the report with the mistakes circled. The Fair Credit Reporting Act says I should only have to wait 30 days for the investigation to be finished. It has been more than 30 days and I still have not heard anything.

I'm guessing that since you have not responded that you were not able to verify the information on the mistaken accounts. Since it has been more than 30 days, please remove the mistakes from my credit report and send me a copy of my updated credit report. Also, as required by law, please send an updated copy of my credit report to anyone who requested a copy of my credit file in the past six months.

Looking forward to hearing from you as I am actively looking for a new job and wouldn't want these mistakes on my credit report to stand in my way.

Sincerely,

{Your signature}

{Your Printed Name}

{Your Address}

{Your Phone Number}

{Your Social Security Number}

Attach a copy of the credit report showing which accounts you are disputing

Attach a copy of your original letter

Attach a copy of the registered letter receipts showing the date they received your original letter

Letter #3: Request for Removal of Negative Items from Original Creditor

{Name of Creditor}

{Address}

{Date}

{Name on account}

To whom it may concern:

On {Date of Credit Report} I received a copy of my credit report which contains errors that are damaging to my credit score. I am requesting the following items be completely investigated as each account contains several mistakes.

{Description of item(s) you are disputing/account number(s)}

I have enclosed a duplicate of the credit report and have highlighted the account(s) in question.

Thank you in advance for your time. I understand that you need to check on these accounts and that you will make sure every detail is accurate. I also understand that under the Fair Credit Reporting Act you will need to complete your investigation within 30 days of receiving this letter. Once you are finished with your investigation, please alert all major credit bureaus where you have reported my information. Also, please send me a letter confirming the changes.

Looking forward to hearing from you as I am actively looking for a new job and wouldn't want these mistakes on my credit report to stand in my way.

Sincerely,

{Your signature}

{Your Printed Name}

{Your Address}

{Your Phone Number}

{Your Social Security Number}

Attach a copy of the credit report showing which accounts you are disputing

Letter #4: If You Don't Receive a Response from Letter #3

{Name of Creditor}

{Address}

{Date}

{Name on account}

To whom it may concern:

On {Date of your first letter} I sent you a letter asking you to investigate several mistakes on my credit report. I've included a copy of my first letter and a copy of the report with the mistakes circled. The Fair Credit Reporting Act says I should only have to wait 30 days for the investigation to be finished. It has been more than 30 days and I still have not heard anything.

I'm guessing that since you have not responded that you were not able to verify the information on the mistaken accounts. Since it has been more than 30 days, please immediately report the updated information to all major credit bureaus so they may update my credit report. Also, please send me a letter confirming these changes to the way you report my account.

Looking forward to hearing from you as I am actively looking for a new job and wouldn't want these mistakes on my credit report to stand in my way.

Sincerely,

{Your signature}

{Your Printed Name}

{Your Address}

{Your Phone Number}

{Your Social Security Number}

Attach a copy of the credit report showing which accounts you are disputing

Attach a copy of your original letter

Attach a copy of the registered letter receipts showing the date they received your original letter

Letter #5: If the Credit Bureau Doesn't Remove Negative Items Disputed

{Name of Credit Bureau}

{Address}

{Date}

{Name on account}

{Report number}

To whom it may concern:

On {Date of your first letter} I sent you a letter asking you to investigate several mistakes on my credit report. I've included a copy of my first letter and a copy of the report with the mistakes circled. According to your response, you have chosen to leave these negative items on my credit report adding insult to injury. The items in question are:

{Creditor 1 / Account number}

{Creditor 2 / Account number}

{Creditor 3 / Account number}

I find it completely unacceptable that you and the creditor refuse to investigate my dispute properly. Your refusal to follow the Fair Credit Reporting Act is causing me untold stress and anxiety. Since you won't follow through, I want to know exactly how you investigated each account. Therefore, I would like the name, title, and contact information of the person at the creditor with whom you did the investigation. This will let me personally follow up with the creditor and find out why they are choosing to report these mistakes on my credit month after month.

I see I am only one person among thousands or more that you have to look after, but to me, this is both personally damaging and humiliating. You may not understand it and you don't have to—all I'm asking is that when people look at my credit file, they see the most accurate information and that's not what's happening.

Please provide me with the requested information right away so I can finally put this nightmare behind me.

Looking forward to hearing from you as I am actively looking for a new job and wouldn't want these mistakes on my credit report to stand in my way.

Sincerely,

{Your signature}

{Your Printed Name}

{Your Address}

{Your Phone Number}

{Your Social Security Number}

Attach a copy of the credit report showing which accounts you are disputing

Attach a copy of your original letter

Attach a copy of the Bureau's response showing no changes to your credit

Letter #6: Affidavit of Unknown Inquiries

EQUIFAX

P.O. box 740256

ATLANTA GA 30374

My name Is John William; my current address is 6767. W Phillips Road, San Jose, CA 78536, SSN: 454-02-9928, Phone: 415-982-3426, Birthdate: 6-5-1981

I checked my credit reports and noticed some inquiries from companies that I did not give consent to access my credit reports; I am very concerned about all activity going on with my credit reports these days. I immediately demand the removal of these inquiries to avoid any confusion as I DID NOT initiate these inquires or give any form of consent electronically, in person, or over the phone. I am fully aware that without permissible purpose no entity is allowed to pull my credit unless otherwise noted in section 604 of the FCRA.

The following companies did not have permission to request my credit report:

CUDL/FIRST CALIFORNIA ON 6-15-2017

CUDL/NASA FEDERAL CREDIT UNION ON 6-15-2017

LOANME INC 3-14-2016

CBNA on 12-22-2017

I once again demand the removal of these unauthorized inquiries immediately.

THANK YOU

(Signature)

Letter #7: Affidavit of Suspicious Addresses

1-30-2018

ASHLEY WHITE

2221 N ORANGE AVE APT 199

FRESNO CA 93727

PHONE: 559-312-0997

SSN: 555-59-4444

BIRTHDATE: 4-20-1979

EQUIFAX

P.O. box 740256

ATLANTA GA 30374

To whom it may concern:

I recently checked a copy of my credit report and noticed some addresses reporting that do not belong to me or have been obsolete for an extended period of time. For the safety of my information, I hereby request that the following obsolete addresses be deleted from my credit reports immediately;

4488 N white Ave apt 840 Fresno, CA 93722

4444 W Brown Ave apt 1027 Fresno CA 93722

13330 E Blue Ave Apt 189 Fresno CA 93706

I have provided my identification card and social security card to verify my identity and current address. Please notify any creditors who may be reporting any unauthorized past accounts that are in connection with these mentioned addresses as I have exhausted all of my options with the furnishers.

(Your signature)

This letter is to get a response from the courts to show the credit bureaus that you have evidence that they cannot legally validate the Bankruptcy

Letter #8: Affidavit of Bankruptcy

U.S BANKRUPTCY COURT

700 STEWART STREET 6301

SEATTLE, WA 98101

RE: BANKRUPTCY (164444423TWD SEATTLE, WA)

To whom it may concern:

My Name is JAMES ROBERT my mailing address is 9631 s 2099h CT Kent, WA 99999.

I recently reviewed my credit reports and came upon the above-referenced public record. The credit agencies have been contacted and they report in their investigation that you furnished or reported to them that the above matter belongs to me. This act may have violated federal and Washington state privacy laws by submitting such information directly to the credit agencies, Experian, Equifax, and Transunion via mail, phone, or fax.

I wish to know if your office violated Washington State and federal privacy laws by providing information on the above-referenced matter via phone, fax, or mail to Equifax, Experian, or TransUnion.

Please respond as I have included a self-addressed envelope,

Thank You

(Your signature)

Letter #9: Affidavit of Erroneous Entry

Dispute letter for bankruptcy to credit bureaus

1-1-18

JAMES LEE

131 S 208TH CT

KENT WA 98031

SSN: 655-88-0000

PHONE: 516-637-5659

BIRTHDATE: 10-29-1985

EXPERIAN

P. O. Box 4500

Allen, TX 75013

RE: BANKRUPTCY (132323993TWD SEATTLE, WA)

To whom it may concern:

My Name is James LEE my mailing address is 131 s 208th CT Kent, WA 98031

I recently disputed the entry of bankruptcy that shows on my credit report which concluded as a verified entry by your bureau. I hereby request your methods of verification, if my request cannot be met, I demand that you delete this entry right away and submit me an updated credit report showing the changes.

Thank You

(Your signature)

Letter #10: Affidavit for Account Validation

First letter you send to the credit bureaus for disputes

1-18-2019

TRANSUNION

P.O. BOX 2000

CHESTER PA 19016

To Whom It May Concern:

My name is John Doe, SSN: 234-76-8989, my current address is 4534. N Folk Street Victorville, CA 67378, Phone: 310-672-0929, and I was born on 4-22-1988.

After checking my credit report, I have found a few accounts listed above that I do not recognize. I understand that before any account or information can be furnished to the credit bureaus; all information and all accounts must be 100% accurate, verifiable, and properly validated. I am not disputing the existence of this debt, but I am denying that I am the responsible debtor. I am also aware that mistakes happen, I believe these accounts can belong to someone else with a similar name or with my information used without my consent either from the furnisher itself or an individual.

I am demanding physical documents with my signature or any legally binding instruments that can prove my connection to these erroneous entries, Failure to fully verify that these accounts are accurate is a violation of the FCRA and must be removed or it will continue to damage my ability to obtain additional credit from this point forward.

I hereby demand that the accounts listed above be legally validated or be removed from my credit report immediately.

Thank You

(Your signature)

Letter #11: Affidavit of Request for Method Verification

Second letter to Credit Bureau if they verified anything

10-22-17

JOSHUA ETHAN

2424 E Dawn Hill way

Merced, CA 93245

SSN: 555-22-3333

Phone: 415-222-9090

Birthdate: 9-29-1987

EQUIFAX

P.O. BOX 740256

ATLANTA GA 30374

To whom it may concern:

I recently submitted a request for investigation on the following accounts which were determined as verified:

Acct Numbers# (XXXXXXX COLLECTION AGENCY A)

(XXXXXXX COLLECTION AGENCY B)

I submitted enough information for you to carry out a reasonable investigation of my dispute, you did not investigate this account or account(s) thoroughly enough as you chose to verify the disputed items.

Under section 611 of the FCRA, I hereby request the methods in which you verified these entries. If you cannot provide me with a reasonable reinvestigation and the methods of which you used for verification, please delete these erroneous entries from my credit report. Furthermore, I would like to be presented with all relevant documents pertaining to the disputed entries.

I look forward to resolving this manner

(Your signature)

Letter #12: Affidavit for Validation

This is the first letter sent to the collection agency if the account is already on your credit reports

1-22-2017

JAMES DANIEL

13233 ROYAL LANDS

LAS VEGAS NV 89141

SSN: 600-60-0003

BIRTHDATE: 2-18-1991

PHONE: 702-331-3912

EXPERIAN

P. O. BOX 4500

ALLEN, TX 75013

To Whom It May Concern:

After reviewing my credit reports, I noticed this unknown item that you must have furnished in error, I formally deny being responsible for any parts of this debt.

Please send me any and all copies of the original documentation that legally binds me to this account, also including the true ownership of this debt.

This account is unknown to me and I formally ask that your entity cease all reporting of this account to the credit agencies and cease all collection attempts.

ACCOUNT: UNIVERSITY OF PHOENIX (IRN 9042029892)

If you cannot present what I request, I demand you stop reporting this account to the credit bureaus to avoid FCRA and FDCPA violations and cease all contact efforts and debt collection activity.

Please respond in writing within 30 days so we can resolve this matter without any more violations.

Thank you. (Your signature)

Chapter 6: How to Avoid Wrong Inquiries

Negative aspects of your credit report are ill-fated blatant prompts of your past financial errors. Or, in some instances, the mistake is not yours, but the company or credit bureau is to blame for the mistakes in the credit report. Either means, it's up to you to operate to delete negative credit report entries from your credit report.

Eliminating derogatory details will aid you to reach a higher credit score. A stronger credit report is also the secret to getting accepted for credit cards and loans and to getting decent interest rates on the accounts that you have accepted. To assist you in getting better credit, here are several methods to delete negative credit report information from your credit report.

Hard Inquiries

Whenever a potential lender or a creditor asks to look into your credit report, it raises an inquiry with the credit bureau. The same will reflect in your report. There are two types of inquiries, either hard or soft inquiries.

If you apply for a line of credit and the lender checks your credit report to decide if you are a potential candidate, is a hard inquiry. A hard inquiry will always show up on your credit report. A hard inquiry will affect your overall credit score. If you apply for a mortgage, credit card, auto loan, or any other form of credit, the lender will check your credit report and score. The lender does this with your permission. They will check your credit report with one or all of the major credit bureaus. Since this inquiry is related to a credit application, they are hard inquiries and will show up in your credit report. And since they show up on your credit report, it will influence your credit score.

Now, let us look at the way hard inquiries affect your credit report. If there are too many hard inquiries about your credit report within a short period, then it is a red flag for potential lenders. Hard inquiries, especially multiple ones, can imply that you are looking to open multiple new accounts. If you start opening multiple accounts, it shows that you are in dire need of funds and that your financial position is not that good. It might also mean that you are overspending. So, it harms your credit report as well as your credit score.

You might be thinking that a person might make multiple inquiries about credit because he is shopping for the best deal on a loan. Credit rating models do consider this possibility. Most will accommodate multiple inquiries made within a short time frame for a line of credit involving a mortgage or a car loan. Numerous inquiries made about a specific credit product will be treated as a single inquiry and will have a relatively smaller effect on your credit report. Usually, you will not be denied credit because of the number of hard inquiries on your credit report. It is because a hard inquiry is only one of the many factors that are taken into consideration for generating your credit report as well as credit score.

Hard inquiries can stay on your credit report for around two years, but as time passes by, their effect also reduces. Even if you have several hard inquiries within a short period, this cannot be a reason for disqualifying you for credit by a lender. Your credit history, as well as the promptness of payments, is the other factors that are taken into consideration before you are either approved or rejected for a loan.

If the hard inquiry in the credit report is accurate, then you cannot have it removed. However, you can dispute a hard inquiry if it was started without your permission or if there was an error. If you notice a hard inquiry from an unfamiliar lender in your credit report, it is something you must look into immediately. It is often a sign of identity theft. So, if you find any inaccurate hard inquiries in your credit report, then you can raise a dispute about them. Upon investigation, if the bureau realizes that the hard inquiry was indeed inaccurate, then it will be removed from your report. When this happens, its effect will also be removed from your credit score.

Soft Inquiries

A soft inquiry occurs whenever you check your credit report. It also happens when you allow someone else to check your credit reports, like a potential employer or a landlord. At times, different businesses, as well as financial institutions, have certain offers that they think will be helpful to you. In such cases, they will check your credit report for pre-approving you for any of those offers. This is also an example of a soft inquiry.

Since a soft inquiry does not directly relate to the application for a new line of credit, they are not usually visible on your credit report. However, there are certain exceptions to this rule. You are the only one who can view the soft inquiries. The two exceptions to this rule are as follows.

- An insurance company might be able to see the inquiries made about you by other similar companies.

- Any inquiry made by debt settlement agencies can be shared with your existing creditors. This can happen only with your prior authorization.

Since there never factored into the credit scoring models, they will not have any effect on your credit report. They are available for reference, but you cannot dispute soft inquiries except for the two mentioned above, soft inquiries cannot be viewed by anyone else.

Managing Inquiries

If you are worried that the hard inquiries are hurting your credit score, then you can take the following steps.

- Be prudent and apply for credit only when needed.
- If you are looking for a specific credit line like a mortgage or auto loan, then you do your rate shopping in a short period.
- Keep checking your credit report regularly to ensure that there are no inaccurate hard inquiries on it.
- Start managing the other important factors that influence your credit score.

If a hard inquiry took place without your approval, then you can remove it from your credit history. If you had no prior knowledge of the hard inquiry made about your credit report or your credit profile, then you have the right to have it removed. At times, you can also get these inquiries removed from the credit report that has been made because you were pressured into accepting an application process that you were not interested in. Here are all the instances of hard inquiries that you can remove from your credit report.

- Any inquiry that was made without your prior knowledge.

- Any inquiry that was made without your consent.
- Any inquiry that was made because you were pressured.

The number of inquiries in your report exceeds the actual amount made.

If you notice an inaccurate hard inquiry on your credit report, then you can send a letter contacting the appropriate agency for its removal. When you are sending a message for removal, you can send it to the credit bureau as well as the lender. Here are the steps you must follow.

The first step is to send a letter for removal of the credit inquiry to the credit bureau and the lender through a certified mail service. A certified mail will record when the letter was sent as well as received. You can use this record as legal proof in case of any discrepancy. This comes in handy, especially when the receiver denies receiving the letter.

Before you send a notice for the removal of your credit inquiries, you need to notify the lender. You are obligated to notify the lender if you wish to take any legal action. Do not be surprised if the lender is not as responsive as the credit bureau. However, this is one step you must not ignore, and it is the right way to go about getting an inaccurate hard inquiry removed from your report.

While you are sending your letter for removal, please ensure that you attach a copy of your credit report with it. Highlight the discrepancy in the report or any other unauthorized inquiries. A credit bureau will have easy access to your account, but it helps investigators if you send a hard copy.

Please ensure that you are sending the letter to the right authority. If the discrepancy was in a report compiled by Equifax, then it does not make any sense to send a copy of the letter to TransUnion. Here are the addresses of the three major credit bureaus in the U.S.

The process of removal of any negative entry from your credit report is lengthy and time-consuming. So, if you like quick results, this process will be a lesson in patience. It might not seem like a couple of points will make much of a difference to your credit score, but they will soon add up to a significant number if left unchecked. Therefore, it is quintessential that you stay on top of any inquiries you make about the removal of negative entries on your credit report. If you want to improve your credit score and want to keep it high, and then ensure that all the entries in your credit report are correct.

- Notes: Making multiple hard inquiries within a short period is usually an indication of filing for bankruptcy. Numerous hard inquiries signify that you are running out of funds or have already run out of funds. It also shows that your financial position is highly unstable. If a person is looking for multiple means of credit at the same time for different reasons, it is an indication of bankruptcy. So, if you are making any hard inquiries within a short period, be mindful of this.

Chapter 7: Frequently Asked Questions about Credit Score

Can Credit Scores Change Very Much Over Time?

In general, ratings do not adjust significantly over time. It's important to remember, though, that your credit score is measured each time it's requested, whether by you or a lender.

What Are the Minimal Requirements for a Credit Score?

To obtain a valid Score, the credit report must include at least one account that has been open for six months or longer, and at least one account registered to a credit bureau during the last six months, and there is no sign of a deceased individual on the credit report

What Are the Various Types of Late Payments and How Do They Affect My Credit Score?

Late payments are considered by the FICO Score based on the following general criteria:

- How recent the late payments are
- How serious the late payments are
- How often the late payments occur.

How Do I Reduce the Negative Impact of Bankruptcy?

A bankruptcy will be factored into your ratings before it is removed from your credit sheet. While it will take up to ten years for a bankruptcy to be removed from the record, the effect of the bankruptcy may diminish over time.

Collections—How Should I Deal with Them and What Do They Do to My Credit?

Collections occur when a bill is 120 days past due. The presence of collections on your credit report would almost definitely lower your Scores.

How Do I Go About Establishing a Credit History?

It can be intimidating to begin building a credit background if you are new to credit. To generate a Score, you must have at least one account that has been open for six months or longer and at least one account that has been reporting to credit bureaus for the last six months.

How Do Lenders Use FICO Scores in the Context of Credit Scores?

FICO Scores assist lenders in evaluating the financial risk of prospective applicants in a timely, reliable, and impartial manner. When you apply for credit or a loan, the lender will almost always use your FICO Scores to determine whether to accept you and what terms and rates you qualify for.

How Can I Obtain a Free Credit Report and Credit Score from Each Bureau?

According to the Fair Credit Reporting Act (FCRA), one of the three credit bureaus is required to provide customers with one free credit report per year.

How Long Can Negative Information on My Credit Report Remain?

It is dependent on the nature of the negative information.

- Hard Inquiries: 2 years
- Late payments: 7 years
- Foreclosures: 7 years
- Collections: 7 years
- Bankruptcies: 7 to 10 years

Can I Improve My FICO Score if My Only Credit Account Is a Charge Card?

Yes.

Will Closing a Credit Card Account Boost My FICO Score?

No.

What Impact Would the "Credit Squeeze" Have on Me?

Lenders now have less money to deal with than in the past. When this occurs and lenders are forced to offer fewer loans, they may make such loans to borrowers who have the greatest chance of repaying—mostly, those with the highest FICO scores. As a result, it is now more important than ever to ensure that you are managing your credit responsibly.

How Can I Keep My Credit Safe if Disaster Strikes?

Preparing for a natural disaster:

- Be aware of the present credit situation.
- Determine the financial situation.
- Think about setting up automated payments for your goals.

Do you have any kind of overdraft protection?

Look at the credit card over-limit guidelines and insurance plans.

What Exactly Are Inquiries, and How Do They Affect My FICO Score?

When you file for credit, you give lenders permission to request or "inquire" for a copy of your credit record from a credit bureau. Credit inquiries are classified into two categories. Viewing your credit report, for example, would not change your FICO Score. Hard inquiries, for instance getting a new mortgage or credit card, can distress your credit score.

Would Getting My Credit Reports Harm or Lower My Credit Score?

A soft pull credit inquiry by a third party of your choosing or a free annual credit report from a government-approved portal. A soft question would not change your credit score because you are not requesting a credit line or loan and are simply doing it for personal reasons.

Does Paying My Bills to Help My Credit?

Regrettably, the credit reporting system does not operate in this manner. When you pay off your mortgage, the unfavorable credit listing does not go away.

Would a Charge Off or a Collection Account Be Removed from My Credit Report if I Pay It Off?

A collection account that has been paid in full also shows up as a collection account on the ledger, so it now has a zero balance.

Is Credit Repair Simple? Will Consumers Do It on Their Own?

It is feasible, but you must be able to put in the effort to master the procedures, accept the dangers of inexperience, and accept that it will most likely take much longer.

Are the Credit Bureaus a Government Branch?

Credit bureaus are for-profit firms. They are not any sort of government agency. They are, though, one of the most highly regulated sectors.

If I Successfully Delete a Negative Item from My Credit Report, Will It Reappear on My Report?

If the credit grantor has not been contacted for 30 days after an item has been challenged, the credit bureaus will sometimes delete the negative listing.

Is It Legal for Creditors to Exclude a Negative, Accurate Listing from My Credit Report? Is It True That Items Remain on the Credit Report for Seven Years?

This is not correct—there is no provision for anything to remain on the credit report. The statute prohibits negative information from appearing for more than seven to ten years.

Chapter 8:   Goodwill Letters

Goodwill letters are not a guaranteed method of removing negative information from your credit report but are still worth a try in some situations. They are more effective if you have a good history with the company; have had a technical error delayed your payment, or if your auto pays did not go through. You can sometimes even convince a credit company to forgive a late payment if you simply forgot to pay.

Try to contact your credit agency by phone to negotiate and explain your situation before sending a goodwill letter. This tactic might be all that you need to do in order to remove the record of the late payment. The sooner you contact, the better as well. If you notice that you have a late payment, calling right away could stop it from being reported at all.

To write a goodwill letter you should:

- Use courteous language that reflects your remorse for the late payment and thank the company for its service.
- Include reasons you need to have the record removed such as qualifying for a home or auto loan or insurance.
- Accept that you were at fault for the late payment.
- Explain what caused the payment to be made late.

To write a goodwill letter you should not:

- Be forceful, rude, or flippant about the situation.

Goodwill Letter Template

Date.

Your name.

Your address.

Your city, state, zip code.

Name of the credit company.

Address.

City, state, zip code.

Re: account number.

Dear Sir or Madam,

Thank you (company's name) for your continued service. I am writing in regard to an urgent request concerning a trade line on my credit reports that I would like to have reconsidered. I have taken pride in making my payments on time and in full since I received (name of credit line/card) on (the date that you received the credit). Unfortunately, I was unable to pay on time (date of missed payment(s)) due to (detailed and personal reason for not being able to pay on time). (You might want to include several sentences using as much information as possible to plead your case.)

(Follow up your reason for not paying on time with a concession of guilt such as:) I have come to see that despite (reason listed above); I should have been better prepared/more responsible with my finances to ensure the payment was on time. I have worked on (some type of learning or way of improving your situation) to prevent this situation from happening again.

I am in need of/about to apply for (new credit line such as a home loan) and it has come to my attention that the notation on my credit report of (credit company's) late payment may prevent me from qualifying or receiving the best interest rates. Since this notation is not a reflection of my status with (Credit Company), I am requesting that you please give me another chance at a positive credit rating by revising my trade lines.

If you need any additional documentation or information from me to reach a positive outcome, please feel free to contact me.

Thank you again for your time,

Sincerely yours,

Your name

(Your signature)

Cease and Desist Letters

The reasons that you might want to send a cease-and-desist letter and the pros and cons of doing so were explained. You want to include your contact information and the account number that you want to stop being contacted about. Use this as a last resort for stopping collection companies as it can backfire, leading to your case being brought to court. Writing a cease-and-desist letter is quite different from writing a dispute letter. Pay attention to their differences.

To make a cease-and-desist letter you should:

- Use professional yet firm language.
- Reference the Fair Debt Collections Practice Act (FDCPA).
- Keep all original copies for your records.
- Send your letter via certified mail.

To make a cease-and-desist letter you should not:

- Incriminate yourself in anything that the collection agency might have accused you of doing.
- Use personal language.

Cease and Desist Letter Template

Date.

Your name.

Your address.

Your city, state, zip code.

Name of the collection agency.

Address.

City, state, zip code.

Re: account number.

To (name of collection agency),

Under the Fair Debt Collections Practices Act (FDCPA), public laws 95–109 and 99–361, I am formally notifying you to cease all communications with me regarding my debt for this account and any other debts that you have purported that I owe.

I will file an objection with the Federal Trade Commission and the (your state) Attorney General's office as well as pursue criminal and civil claims against you and your company if you attempt to continue contacting me after you receive this notice. If I receive any further communications after you have confirmed receipt of this notice, the communications may be recorded as evidence for my claims against you.

You should also be aware that any negative information related to this account on my credit reports will be handled with all legal rights available to me.

Regards,

Your name

(Your signature)

Chapter 9: More Tips

Tips on Filing a Dispute with Section 609

You will want to make sure everything is done correctly, as this will make it more likely that the information will come off, and no one will place it back on your report again.

- Make the necessary changes to the letter. This will include changing the name and address. You will also want to make sure your phone number is included. Sometimes people include their email addresses, but this is not necessary. It is always safer to only include your home address or P.O. Box information. You will also want to make sure to edit the whole letter if something does not match up to what you want to say in your message, such as what you are trying to dispute on your credit report. These letters are quite generic, which means you need to add information related to you.
- You want to make sure that all the account information you want to be taken off your credit report is handwritten. You also want to make sure you use blue ink rather than black. On top of this, you do not need to worry about being too neat, but you want to make sure they can read the letters and numbers correctly. This is an essential part of filing your dispute letter because handwritten ones in blue ink will not be pushed through their automated system.
- They have an automatic mode that will read the letter for them and punch in the account number you use. They will then send you a generic message that states these accounts are now off your credit report, which does not mean that it

happened. When you write the information down, a person needs to read it and will then take care of it.

- You want to make sure that you prove who you are with your letters. While this is never an easy thing to do, you must send a copy of your social security card and your driver's license, or they will shred your letter. You also need to make sure that you get each of your messages notarized. You can typically do this by visiting your county's courthouse.
- You can send as many letters as you need to; however, keep in mind that the creditor typically will not make you submit more than four. This is because when you threaten to take them to court in the third letter, they will realize that your accounts and demands are just not worth it. First, you could damage their reputation, and secondly, you will cost them more money by doing that compared to only taking the information off your credit report.
- You will want to make sure that you keep all correspondence they send you. Many people struggle to get them to pay attention because that is just how the system works. Therefore, you need to make sure that you do not listen to their quick automatic reply that your information is of your credit report. You also want to make sure to wait at least three months and then re-run your credit report to make sure the wrong information has been removed. Keep track of every time you need to re-run your credit report as you can use this as proof if they continue to send you a letter stating the information is off of your credit report.

However, this is a new system, which means that it does come with more problems than sending one through the mail. While it is ultimately your choice whether you use a form to fill you always want to make sure you keep copies and continue to track them, even if you don't hear from the credit bureau after a couple of months. It will never hurt to send them a second letter or even a third.

The Necessary Documents before Sending the Letter

One wellspring of income for them originates from selling the information on our credit reports to different lenders, managers, insurance agencies, credit card organizations, and those you approve of to see your credit information. In addition to the fact that they provide raw data, they likewise sell them using various methods for examining the data to decide the risk of stretching out credit to us. In addition to trading our information to lenders, they likewise sell our data to us. Credit scores, credit observing administrations, extortion security, and wholesale fraud prevention—interestingly enough, this region has quickly gotten perhaps the most significant wellspring of income. Furthermore, those pre-endorsed offers in our letter drop each week or garbage mail? That is right; they got our information from the credit bureaus as well. Organizations buy into assistance provided by the three credit bureaus that sell a rundown of consumer's credit information that fits pre-decided criteria.

Presently, as opposed to prevalent thinking, credit bureaus do not have any contribution. However, by utilizing the entirety of the set information on your credit report (personal information, payment history, and credit propensities) and FICO's technique for scoring that data, they tell them how creditworthy you are.

Where to Send Your 609 Letters?

Credit bureaus collect information from various sources following consumer information. The activity is done for multiple reasons and includes data from singular consumers. Included is the information concerning a person's charge payments and their getting. Utilized for evaluating creditworthiness, the info provides lenders with an outline of your accounts if a loan repayment is required. The interest rates charged on loans are additionally worked out concerning the kind of credit score shown by your experience. It is like this, not a uniform procedure, and your credit report is a vital instrument that affects future loans.

Based on risk-based valuing, it pegs various risks on multiple customers in this manner, deciding the cost you will acquire as a borrower. Done as a credit rating, it is assistance provided to various interested parties in the public. Terrible credit histories are affected for the most part by settled court commitments, which mark you for high-interest rates every year. Duty liens and bankruptcies, for example, shut you out of the conventional credit lines and may require a great deal of arrangement for any loan to be offered by the bank.

Bureaus collect and examine credit information, including financial data, personal information, and elective data. Various sources give this generally marked data furnishers. These have an exceptional association with the credit bureaus. An average gathering of data furnishers would comprise creditors, lenders, utilities, and debt collection agencies. Pretty much any association which has had payment involvement in the consumer is qualified, including courts.

Any data collected for this situation is provided to the credit bureaus for grouping. When it is accumulated, the data is placed into specific repositories and files claimed by the bureau. The information is made accessible to customers upon request. The idea of such information is necessary for lenders and managers.

The information is in this manner material in various conditions; credit evaluation and business thoughts are simply part of these. The consumer may likewise require the data to check their score, and the home proprietor may need to check their inhabitant's report before renting an apartment. Since borrowers saturate the market, the ratings will, in general, be robotic. A straightforward examination would deal with this by giving the client a calculation for rapid appraisal and checking your score once every other year to deal with errors in your report.

Individuals from the public are qualified for one free credit report from every one of the significant bureaus. Business reports, for example, Paid, might be gotten on request and are chargeable. Lawful expressions for the credit bureaus incorporate Credit Report Agency or CRA in the U.S. This is organized in the Fair Credit Report Act or FCTA. Other government rules associated with the assurance of the consumer incorporate the Fair and Accurate Credit Transaction Act, Fair Credit Billing Act, and Regulation B. Statutory bodies have additionally been made for the regulation of the credit bureaus. The Fair-Trade Commission serves as a controller for the consumer credit report agencies. At the same time, the Office of the Comptroller of Currency fills in as a manager of all banks going about as furnishers.

Tips for Letter Writing

If you send a credit claim letter to a credit office, you first need to locate your credit report—this can be a bigger task than it seems, particularly since the credit office in question may have reported about almost everybody in the world reporting on it. You will need to provide detail on the mistake after you have found the submission, as well as a clarification as to why you are disputing the object. Eventually, the payment claim letter should include a request to remove the object from the credit report to the credit bureau.

It should have what it needs to decide on your case by providing the bureau with the necessary information.

Here's what to include:

- Updated date
- The particulars (name, contact information, date of birth, and account number)
- Contact information for the Credit office
- A brief description of the mistake (no need for a long and complicated tale to regale them)
- Any documentation you might have that can help prove your point, such as payment records or court documents (be sure to mention in the letter why you submitted them)

Notes on what you want the credit office to do (re-examine and delete the element from your report)

- A duplicate of the credit report labeled with a mistake

- A scanned copy of your Government ID (such as your driver's license) and a bill or other paper showing your identity

Here are just a few samples of arguable products:

- Collections
- Late payments
- Bankruptcies not stopped until 7 to 10 years
- Pre-closures not lifted until seven years

609 letters are a perfect place to theoretically clear out a few derogatory things that you were not able to delete earlier from your credit report. Even though these are your items, creditors must register them properly and be ready to show them.

Chapter 10: How to Reach 800+ Credit Score

Now it is time for the hard part. Maybe you have been doing some of the work that we go through in this guidebook, and you have seen a nice increase in the amount of your FICO score.

This is always good news, but now we want to see further if we can get our score to 800 or higher. Only the elite have this kind of score. It is hard to get it because it requires a perfect balance of credit types, a high credit limit, and no missed payments, among other things. But it is possible.

When you can get your credit to be this high, it is a lot easier for you to go through and actually get credit and loans at any time you would like. If something happens and you have many medical bills to deal with, then this credit score can help you take care of that. It can also be used for non-emergencies as well like if you would like to start a business, get a new house, or do something else along the same lines.

So, how do you make sure that you can get your credit score up to 800 or higher? The first thing is to know the facts. Once you are able to answer the main question of "What is a perfect credit score?" you will find that it is easier to take on the right steps to figure out exactly what you can do to reach the perfect score. First, though, you need to make sure you know where you stand on the FICO scale.

Once a year, you can get a free annual credit report from any of the country's top credit bureaus, all three of them. If you go through this and find any issues on any of them (sometimes a mistake will show up on one and not on the others), then this is the time to fix them. You will never get to an 800+ score if there are a bunch of errors in your report.

The next thing that you can focus on is establishing a long history of credit.

Most of the time, with a few exceptions, lenders are going to view borrowers with short histories of credit as riskier to work with. To reach a credit score that is 800 or higher, you have to establish, and then also maintain a long history. So even if you are not using some of the accounts, keeping them open will help you to get that score up.

As we have mentioned a bit before, you need to make sure that all of your bills are paid on time. There isn't a single person who has an 800+ credit score who also has a missed payment, or a bunch of missed payments, on their report. Paying your bills late or not paying the bills at all is going to decrease your score. If you have trouble remembering the due dates, then consider signing up so for automatic payments and have that taken care of for you.

You also need to take the time to redefine your credit card usage. About 30 percent of the score, you have will consist of the utilization rate for your credit, which is going to be the amount of debt you owe divided by the total credit available. Typically, we want to stay under 30 percent, but if you are trying to get a higher score, then staying under 10 percent is best.

One thing that we have not talked about much in this guidebook yet but that will help you to get that higher score you want, is to learn how to diversify the accounts that you are holding onto. This is one of the best ways to strengthen your credit, and while it can take some time to accomplish this, you will find it is a great way for us to make sure your credit score is able to go up.

You can make your credit score stronger when you can diversify your accounts. This is not an excuse to go out there and open up 10 different card accounts at a time. What it means is that you should have a mix of different types of credit, such as an auto loan, a student loan, a mortgage, and a credit card. Ten credit cards are not going to be a diverse mix of debt or show responsibility with your score. But having a bunch of different accounts, even if some of them have been paid off, is going to be a much better option to work with.

While you work on your credit score, you need to make sure that you cut your spending and create a budget that you are able to stick with. This helps you to stay within means that you can afford and makes it less likely that you are going to fall into trouble with your spending. Although, indeed, your credit is not going to factor in your income, living within your means, no matter what that number is, is a great way to raise your score.

Next on the list is to find ways that you can limit the liability that you are dealing with. When you go to co-sign a loan, remember that this may seem like a nice thing to do, but you are really taking on a risk for another person. If you do this for someone who is not able to manage their debt all that well, it is going to negatively affect your score because you will be responsible for that debt as well.

In addition to this, you should make sure that your liability is limited in other manners as well. You should always report cards that have been lost or stolen right away. If you don't do this, then it is likely that you will be liable for any of the purchases that are not authorized at the time. And if you are not able to afford those purchases, then your score is going to be the thing that suffers here.

And finally, you need to make sure that you are restricting the hard inquiries that happen to your report. Whether it is you or another agency or institution that is pulling out the credit report and asking for a copy of it, you are dealing with an inquiry. A soft inquiry can happen on occasion, and it is generally not going to be enough to make any changes to your credit. This soft inquiry is going to happen when one of the following occurs:

- You go through and do a check on your own credit report.
- You give an employer you may work with in the future permission to go through and check your credit.
- You have the financial institutions that you do business with go through and check your credit.
- You get a credit card offer that has been preapproved, and that specific company goes through and checks your credit.

While the soft inquiry is not going to do all that much to your credit scores, you do need to be careful about the hard inquiry. This is going to be the one that is able to affect your credit score. This is when a company pulls up your credit report after you apply for a product like a credit card or a mortgage. You want to make sure that you can limit the hard inquiries as much as possible to get the best results with this.

Chapter 11: Credit Repair

Now that you have dealt with any possible errors that might have plagued your credit, you are ready to move on to the tough stuff. This is the stage where you need to review your financial habits and figure out which ones are healthy and which ones are only hurting your credit score. It's not an easy process. Many of the mistakes we make are completely unintentional, but no less harmful to our financial security. Additionally, it can be tough to change the patterns that have long since become ingrained in our daily, weekly, and monthly routines. However, making these changes is necessary if you want to turn your credit around, as you have already seen how it gets with a negatively impacted score. At this point, your only options are to continue allowing your creditworthiness to deteriorate, further putting you into debts as you fail to qualify for credit lines and you get poor interest rates for those you do obtain, or you can make the tough changes that will set you on the path to future financial success.

Repairing your credit starts with making changes to the way you view and interact with your finances. If you continue to put things off, leave debts to pile up, and generally treat your credit like a secondary issue, it will continue to grow worse.

You want to shoot for long-lasting changes in the way you spend your money and the mentality you have when utilizing debt. If you are always looking to be conscientious about your score and your overall financial health, you will find it much easier to stick to making good credit decisions. However, the intention is only half the battle; the other half is learning what to do and getting it done.

If you try to repair your credit though you don't know how to go about doing it, you may waste time and money by failing to put your effort where it is most needed.

As a rule of thumb, target the big stuff first, and then move on to the things that are only having a minimal impact on your credit.

You want to avoid making common credit mistakes that will stagnate your process. Learn what to do and what not to do and you will be halfway to putting this knowledge into practice and enjoying the benefits of an outstanding credit score.

Lifestyle Changes and Financial Strategies

Bringing your credit score up to a healthy number requires you to make some lifestyle changes. You may not be able to make frivolous purchases because you cannot afford to worsen your debt, or because you need to increase the cash you have at hand to pay your debts off. You may also need to adjust the method by which you allocate funds for making payments and the way you utilize available lines of credit. Once you have made the appropriate changes and developed certain financial strategies that will make your relationship with money a much more positive one, you will find it easier to stay on top of credit payments. The following section contains a list of strategies you can use and actions you can take to increase your credit score directly and finally get you out of debt.

Pay Bills on Time

Late payments do your credit score no favors. You must get into the habit of paying your bills on time. Unpaid debts are hard to recover from, and routinely making late payments can make it hard to be on time for future payments. You want to correct these negative habits as soon as possible. If you have the money, but you struggle to get payments in on time, try marking them on your calendar or setting up automatic payments. Try to make payments for a given account at the same time each month. For example, you might make sure you always pay your rent on the 25th of the month, or you might pay your phone bill on the second Tuesday of every month. Once you get into the habit of making a few payments on time, you will be more inclined to remember them at the end of every billing period.

Pay More than the Minimum

If you have the money available, you should try to pay more than your accounts' minimum payment. Having a balance remaining at the end of a payment period lets interest accrue on your debt, which can double or triple the amount you are paying depending on the APR and the cost of the debt. Interest can build up over time into some very steep costs—all the more reason you should avoid only paying the minimum. If you can pay even $10 or $15 more on an account, you can reduce the amount of interest you are charged and keep future payments lower.

Maintain Low Credit Card Balances

Using a large portion of your available credit hurts your credit score. It suggests a dependency on credit and an inability to pay off debts promptly. To counteract this, you should keep the balances on each of your credit cards low compared to your credit limits. You do not necessarily have to pay them off in full but aim to use under 30% of your available credit at any given time for the best credit score results. Many maxed out and nearly maxed out cards on your credit report can seriously hurt your score and make it hard to get approved for future cards.

Pay Maxed-Out Cards First

Like the point above, you should always prioritize any maxed-out cards when deciding what to pay off first. You do not want to have any of your cards hit their credit limit if it is avoidable. Having a maxed-out card impacts your credit score much more severely than even a card that has 90% of its credit limit in use. Always try to pay down these cards before dealing with others, as they can hurt your score when left to linger.

Conclusion

Credit is significant for anybody's accounts. It gives an individual history and reputation of their budgetary history. With credit, individuals can fund things, for example, a house or a vehicle. At whatever point an individual has credit, it is significant that they use it shrewdly. A decent record as a consumer will empower them to get low financing costs on credits just as they can get more cash. There are various things that individuals should remember when utilizing credit. They should do things, for example, take care of tabs on schedule, check their announcements, check their credit reports and maintain a strategic distance from the base installment propensity.

Dealing with your record is significant on the off chance that you need to ensure that you can acquire enough cash to purchase a house or a vehicle. It will likewise enable you to get the most minimal loan costs and set aside your cash thus. At whatever point you are hoping to deal with your credit, it will be imperative to ensure that you charge a sum that you can stand to pay back and take care of your tabs on schedule. This will enable you to build up and keep up a decent record of loan repayment and deal with your credit carefully.

Understanding your credit is the first step to improving it. Hopefully, this book was able to help you do both. While there are now credit repair services, you may end up incurring debts to get them—so do be careful. Furthermore, getting such services will be useless if you don't understand how you landed a terrible credit situation in the first place.

You can improve your credit in many ways. As you learned from this book, it can be as simple as modifying your spending habits or correcting wrong information in your records. It could also be as difficult as paying all your debts at once and dealing with high-interest rates. Don't forget to ditch the services that you thought would be helpful but turned out to be damaging to your finances and credit score.

Being mindful of your credit does a lot of wonders to your financial situation. It trains you to become a wise spender and keeps you away from personal bankruptcy. It also helps ensure that you won't incur debts that you can't handle. Above all, managing your credit will enable you to pursue the life you want.

It may take some time to see significant changes in your credit score. Nevertheless, you can feel some of its advantages as you keep on practicing good financial habits.

You'll need patience in enhancing your credit. After all, you're going to deal with different individuals and institutions in checking your records, correcting wrong information, and borrowing money.

The next step is to find and implement ways to increase your sources of income. You can do so by getting another job, setting up a business, or investing. Make sure you have sources of both active and passive income.

You may use a portion of your savings or credit to finance your new venture. With a good credit score, you can get quick loan approval and a low-interest rate. Just keep in mind to pay your debts on time.

Made in the USA
Coppell, TX
03 August 2024

35548424R00140